What Is Life?

What Is Life?
A Bowl of Cherries and Nearly 800 Other Answers

Compiled and With an Introduction by
Ronald B. Shwartz

A CITADEL PRESS BOOK
Published by Carol Publishing Group

Copyright © 1995 by Ronald B. Shwartz
All rights reserved. No part of this book may be reproduced in any form, except by a newspaper or magazine reviewer who wishes to quote brief passages in connection with a review.

A Citadel Press Book
Published by Carol Publishing Group
Citadel Press is a registered trademark of Carol Communications, Inc.
Editorial Offices: 600 Madison Avenue, New York, N.Y. 10022
Sales and Distribution Offices: 120 Enterprise Avenue, Secaucus, N.J. 07094
In Canada: Canadian Manda Group, One Atlantic Avenue, Suite 105, Toronto, Ontario M6K 3E7
Queries regarding rights and permissions should be addressed to Carol Publishing Group, 600 Madison Avenue, New York, N.Y. 10022

Carol Publishing Group books are available at special discounts for bulk purchases, for sales promotions, fund-raising, or educational purposes. Special editions can be created to specifications. For details, contact Special Sales Department, Carol Publishing Group, 120 Enterprise Avenue, Secaucus, N.J. 07094

Manufactured in the United States of America
10 9 8 7 6 5 4 3 2 1

Library of Congress Cataloging-in-Publication Data
What is Life? : a bowl of cherries and nearly 800 other answers /
    compiled and with an introduction by Ronald B. Shwartz.
      p.   cm.
    "A Citadel Press book."
    ISBN 0–8065–1606–2 (pbk.)
    1. Life—Quotations, maxims, etc.   I. Shwartz, Ronald B.
PN6084.L53W48   1995
082—dc20   94–45482
                                                              CIP

Introduction

It began as a kind of hobby, the gropings of an adolescent steeped in *The Catcher in the Rye* and trying to find out—bottom-line—what life is all about. I knew, of course, that life is not a bowl of cherries or a dress rehearsal, knew it doesn't really start at forty, and knew it isn't merrily or otherwise but a dream. And I knew that nobody gets out of it alive and that whether it's worth living or not has little to do with whether it's unexamined. What I didn't know was, in short, everything else. And because the matter was literally one of life and death I wanted, in the feverish way that only an adolescent can, to find out before it was too late.

There were, for all that, conspicuous limits to this almost Hamlet-like mission of mine. I did not join est or learn yoga, did not seek meaning in Tibet or in hallucinogens, did not revisit the religion stuffed down my gullet at a tender age. Nor did I seek out the fabled wisdom of elders, who seemed at the time none wiser for being older. There were, I recall, some brief flirtations with Nietzsche, and I did try once in college to plow through Sartre's *Being and Nothingness* but I gave up at page six of the Special Abridged Edition. At no time since did I ever aspire to complete The Great Books of Western Civilization or seek my metaphysical way through the *I Ching*.

It seems now that what I craved instead was deep truth more easily attained, the moral equivalent of fast food for thought but subtly seasoned to befit the antic complexity of life in an imperfect world. And I began to find it in epigrams: the meaning of life in a nutshell, glib but suitably oxymoronic precepts on what it's all about, pointed quotations by sages heralded and unheralded. All of them professing to sum up, in a single lapidary sentence or two, the meaning—the consummate nature—of our common existential predicament. What it is, what it isn't, and how to do it, endure it, and exploit it for fun and profit. Metaphors for life, life itself as the supreme metaphor.

As a putative adult, lacking the courage of these early obsessions, I did not take up near Walden or any other pond to live "deliberately"—to borrow Thoreau's immortal adverb—or to "front," as he put it, "the essential facts of life." Instead, in congress with the lemmings of a generation bent on promoting their options not so much for life as for livelihood, I simply went to law school. What I fronted there were not the essential facts of life but merely the essential facts of appellate opinions, whose correspondence to life as I knew it seemed at best coincidental. A decade later, having ended up twenty miles east of Walden (not in a cabin but in a corporate law firm), I was still mining the hills for terse insights into life—wry, rueful, irreverent, and endlessly provocative definitions of life compiled over half a lifetime of reading, research, and serendipity.

This book is the eclectic and largely unpremeditated result of that quest—a private archive that got out of hand. For better or worse it is, so far as I know, the most comprehensive if not only collection of its kind in existence, harvested from well over two thousand quotes from sources old and new, highbrow and low, sacred and profane:

from George Will to Rodney Dangerfield, from Kafka to Khrushchev, Oscar Wilde to Julia Child, Santayana to David Letterman, Gandhi to Gauguin, Robert Frost to Katharine Hepburn, Voltaire to Pavarotti, ex-governor Jerry Brown to ex-Beatle Paul McCartney. And hundreds more, all gleaned from fiction and non-fiction, newspapers, magazines, plays, movies, television, song lyrics, and even the occasional bumper sticker of unknown provenance.

The German playwright Bertoldt Brecht once said that "everything there is to say about life on this planet can be put into a single sentence of average length." This is a debatable proposition and a fragile premise upon which any anthology of wit and wisdom may lay claim to righteous standing in a culture jaded by sound bites. But it's enough that these pithy pronouncements on life may satisfy the most catholic curiosity and are decidedly not of the solemn or sappy "inspirational message" type. Enough to lend interest, amusement, recognition, a sense of wonder and a dollop of enlightenment to even the least philosophically inclined among us.

Boston
July, 1994

What Is Life?

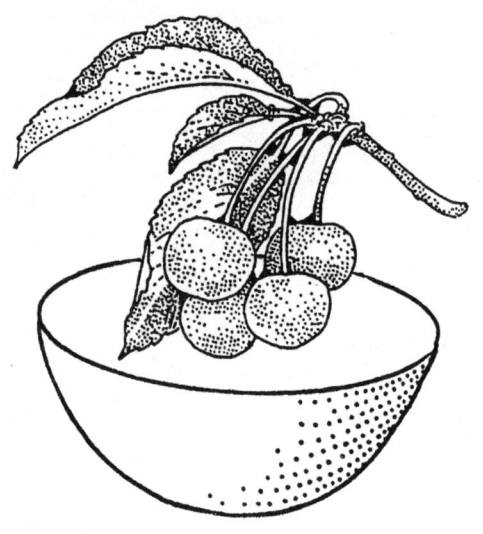

Life is a game, of which the first rule is: This is no game. This is dead serious.
>   ALAN WATTS

We go through life pulling on doors marked "push."
>   OGDEN NASH
>   *Verses From 1929 on,* 1952

Life is made up of sobs, sniffles, and smiles, with sniffles predominating.
>   O. HENRY
>   *The Four Million,* 1906

Life is not a funeral march to the grave. It's a polka.

> DENNIS KUCINICH,
> former Mayor of Cleveland

Life is a tragedy full of joy.

> BERNARD MALAMUD

Life is a business which does not cover expenses.

> ARTHUR SCHOPENHAUER

The first half of life consists of the capacity to enjoy life without the chance, and the last half consists of the chance without the capacity.

> MARK TWAIN

We do not find the deep truths of life. They find us.

> ERNEST HEMINGWAY

Life's not a paragraph/ And death I think is no parenthesis.

> E.E. CUMMINGS
> *is 5*, 1926

There are two great rules of life, the one general and the other particular. The first is that everyone can, in the end, get what he wants if he only tries. This is the general rule. The particular rule is that every individual is, more or less, an exception to the rule.

> SAMUEL BUTLER

My father advised me that life itself was a crap game: it was one of the two lessons I learned as a child. The other was that overturning a rock was apt to reveal a rattlesnake. As lessons go those two seem to hold up, but not to apply.

> JOAN DIDION
> *Play It As It Lays*, 1970

Linus: Life is rarely all one way, Charlie Brown. You win a few, and you lose a few.
Charlie Brown: Really? Gee, that'd be neat.

                                                CHARLES SCHULZ, from *Peanuts*

When we remember that we are all mad, the mysteries disappear and life stands explained.

                                                MARK TWAIN

Life is a long lesson in humility.

                                                JAMES M. BARRIE

If one considered life as a simple loan, one would perhaps be less exacting.

                                                DELACROIX

Life is short. Eat dessert first.

H. BLAND ET AL.
Life is Too Short, 1994

It was previously a question of finding out whether or not life had to have a meaning to be lived. It now becomes clear, on the contrary, that it will be lived all the better if it has no meaning.

> ALBERT CAMUS
> *The Myth of Sisyphus,* 1955

Life is easier to take than you'd think; all that is necessary is to accept the impossible, do without the indispensable, and bear the intolerable.

> KATHLEEN NORRIS

Life to him, as to every other man of large practical knowledge and insight, was an inexplicable tangle.

> THEODORE DREISER
> *The Financier,* 1925

Life is half promise and half threat. It is like Walter Cronkite giving us fair notice that he will be back with more news in a moment.

> an unnamed fictional character
> quoted by GEORGE F. WILL
> *The Pursuit of Happiness and Other Sobering Thoughts*, 1978

The trouble with you, Jenny Blair, is that you do not know the first thing about life. It is only by knowing how little life has in store for us that we are able to look on the bright side and avoid disappointment.

> JENNY'S GRANDMOTHER
> in Ellen Glasgow's *The Sheltered Life*, 1932

Life is a concentration camp. You can only rage impotently against your persecutors.

> WOODY ALLEN

"Life is hard." "Compared to what?"

> SYDNEY J. HARRIS

The whole trouble is that I lived half my life before I found out that it's a do-it-yourself job.

> SOURCE OBSCURE

Life is either a daring adventure, or nothing.

> HELEN KELLER

Life is not a spectacle or a feast; it is a predicament.

> GEORGE SANTAYANA

Life can only be understood backwards, but it must be lived forwards.

> SØREN KIERKEGAARD

Life is like playing a violin solo in public and learning the instrument as one goes on.

          SAMUEL BUTLER

Life is the only sentence which doesn't end with a period.

          LOIS GOULD

In three words I can sum up everything I've learned about life: It goes on.

          ROBERT FROST

There is more to life than increasing its speed.

          MOHANDAS K. GANDHI

Life is offered to you on certain terms. You accept the terms and create the terms, you learn to make love with whatever it is that frightens you.

          JAMES BALDWIN
          quoted in *People* magazine,
          January 7, 1980

Life is like a B-picture script. It is that corny. If I had my life story offered to me to film, I'd turn it down.

> KIRK DOUGLAS
> *Look* magazine, October 4, 1955

Life is seldom as unendurable as, to judge by the facts, it logically ought to be.

> BROOKS ATKINSON
> *Once Around the Sun,* 1951

Life is a toy made of glass; it appears to be of inestimable price, but in reality it is very cheap.

> PIETRO ARETINO
> letter to Bernardo Tasso,
> September 26, 1537

Life is simply one damned thing after another.

> Attributed to ELBERT HUBBARD

Life is like an onion, which one peels crying.
>   FRENCH PROVERB

The basic fact about human existence is not that it is a tragedy, but that it is a bore. It is not so much a war as an endless standing in line.
>   H. L. MENCKEN
>   *Prejudices: Sixth Series,* 1927

Human life is but a series of footnotes to a vast obscure unfinished masterpiece.
>   VLADIMIR NABOKOV
>   *Pale Fire,* 1962

Life is a gamble, at terrible odds—if it was a bet you wouldn't take it.
>   TOM STOPPARD
>   *Rosencrantz and Guildenstern Are Dead,* 1967

Life is the greatest bargain; we get it for nothing.

> YIDDISH PROVERB

Not a shred of evidence exists in favor of the idea that life is serious.

> JOSEPH CAMPBELL, sometimes attributed to Brendan Gill

Life is what happens to us while we are making other plans.

> THOMAS LA MANCE, later attributed to John Lennon

Life is just a bowl of pits.

> RODNEY DANGERFIELD

Life is like a blanket too short. You pull it up and your toes rebel, and you yank it down and shivers meander about your shoulder; but cheerful folks manage to draw their knees up and pass a very comfortable night.

> MARION HOWARD

The first half of our life is ruined by our parents and the second half by our children.

CLARENCE DARROW

My grandfather always said that living is like licking honey off a thorn.

LOUIS ADAMIC

The game of life is not so much in holding a good hand as playing a poor hand well.

T. H. LESLIE

Life is a train, but all the compartments are already filled up, and there is no seat left for the newcomer. When the conductor asks for your ticket—your justification for existing—your pockets are empty (just like everybody else's, but of course you're not aware of that).

JEAN-PAUL SARTRE
Words, 1964

Life is a theatre in which the worst people often have the best seats.

> attributed to ARISTONYMUS by Joannes Stobaeus
> *Florilegium*, c. 500 B.C.

Life is far too important a thing ever to talk seriously about.

> OSCAR WILDE

Life is a fatal complaint, and an eminently contagious one.

> OLIVER WENDELL HOLMES
> *The Poet at the Breakfast-Table*, 1884

Life is not having been told that the man has just waxed the floor.

> OGDEN NASH

Life is a copycat and can be bullied into following the master artist who bids it come to heel.

> HEYWOOD BROUN

Life is a foreign language; all men mispronounce it.
>
> CHRISTOPHER MORLEY
> *Thunder on the Left*, 1925

Life don't run away from nobody. Life runs at people.
>
> JOE FRAZIER
> quoted in *Newsweek* magazine,
> March 18, 1968

Life is the art of drawing sufficient conclusions from insufficient premises.
>
> SAMUEL BUTLER
> *Notebooks*, 1913

We are encamped like bewildered travelers in a garish, unrestful hotel.
>
> JOSEPH CONRAD
> on life, in *Victory*, 1915

Life is a jigsaw puzzle with most of the pieces missing.

> ARAB PROVERB

Life just is. You have to flow with it.

> JERRY BROWN
> former California Governor

One learns in life to keep silent and draw one's own confusions.

> CORNELIA OTIS SKINNER

It is not true that life is one damn thing after another—it's one damn thing over and over.

> EDNA ST. VINCENT MILLAY

A new question has arisen in modern man's mind, the question, namely, whether life is worth living. . . . No sensible answer can be given because the question does not make sense.

> ERICH FROMM

Our whole life is spent sketching an ineradicable portrait of ourselves.

> ANDRE GIDE
> *The Journals of Andre Gide*, 1956

Life is a shit sandwich and every day you take another bite of it.

> JOE SCHMIDT
> American pro football player, 1976

It's rather serious—life. And you can't live as if you have nine lives. I find myself doing that often. I think everybody does, saying in his mind, "I'll get it tomorrow." But I can't do that anymore.

> PAUL MCCARTNEY
> quoted in *Life* magazine,
> April 16, 1971

Life begins at the centerfold and expands outward.

> LISA BAKER
> *Playboy*'s Miss November of 1966

My theory is to enjoy life, but the practice is against it.

> CHARLES LAMB
> *The Letters of Charles and Mary Lamb*, 1912

In life, understanding is the booby prize.

> WERNER ERHARD

There is much talk of the chaotic character of human life. It is, in fact, a tangled growth, but always sequent, always proceeding from roots, like the vines and brambles in the swamp. You may not be able to get through, you may be entangled, lost, destroyed, but the life itself is orderly—delicately, beautifully so, if you could stop to examine it.

> CHARLES HORTON COOLEY
> *Life and the Student*

A little work, a little sleep, a little love, and it is all over.

> MARY ROBERTS RINEHART
> on life

Life is too short to be small.

> BENJAMIN DISRAELI

When I think of all the books I have read, and of the wise words I have heard spoken, and of the anxiety I have given to parents and grandparents, and of the hopes that I have had, all life weighed in the scales of my own life seems to me a preparation for something that never happens.

> W. B. YEATS
> *Autobiography*, 1927

What a rotten writer of detective stories life is.

> NATHAN LEOPOLD
> kidnapper/murderer

Life is like eating artichokes—you've got to go through so much to get so little.

                    T. A. DORGAN

The solution to the problem of life is seen in the vanishing of the problem. Is not this the reason why those who have found after a long period of doubt that the sense of life became clear, have then been unable to say what constituted that sense?

                    LUDWIG WITTGENSTEIN

What is life but a series of inspired follies?

                    GEORGE BERNARD SHAW

Life is always walking up to us and saying "Come on in, the living's fine," and what do we do? Back off and take its picture.

                    RUSSELL BAKER

The first forty years of life give us the text; the next thirty supply the commentary.

> ARTHUR SCHOPENHAUER

The proposition that life is a science is intellectually indefensible; the proposition that life is an art is pragmatically impossible.

> JOSEPH WOOD KRUTCH
> *The Modern Temper,* 1956

Life's a long headache in a noisy street.

> JOHN MASEFIELD
> *The Widow in the Bye Street,* 1912

Life is a zoo in a jungle.

> PETER DE VRIES
> *The Vale of Laughter,* 1967

What's life anyway? A few winters waiting for summer. A few summers wishing they were longer. A few bottles of whiskey and a half dozen women you can remember.

> STEVE
> in Victor Fleming's *The Virginian*

Life would be tolerable were it not for its amusements.

> G. C. LEWIS

Life is absolutely super and wonderful. There shouldn't be any sadness in it. People should be aware of all things at all times; they should experience the extremities of life, fulfill themselves completely. Why does everyone want to go to sleep when the only thing left is to stay awake?

> EDWARD ALBEE
> quoted in the *New York Times*,
> April 18, 1971

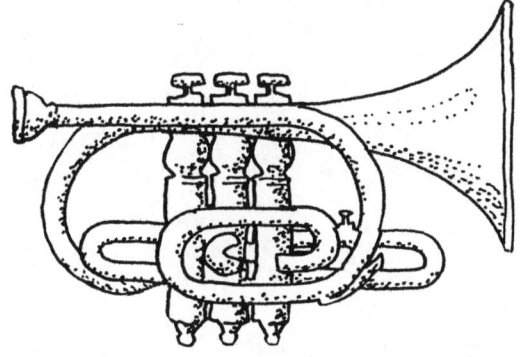

*Life is something like this trumpet.
If you don't put anything in it
you don't get anything out.
And that's the truth.*

W. C. HANDY
jazz musician/composer

Life is like a child's undershirt—short and soiled.

> YIDDISH PROVERB

Life is the most amazing fanfare of purely temporary and always changing and ever vanishing and, in the main, clownish and ever-ridiculous interests that it has ever been my lot to witness.

> quoted without attribution by
> HARRY EMERSON FOSDICK
> *On Being a Real Person,* 1943

Life is the garment we continually alter but which never seems to fit.

> quoted without attribution by
> JACOB M. BRAUDE
> *Source Book for Writers and Speakers,* 1968

What is life for, unless to do at least certain things right?

> JACQUES BARZUN
> *Simple and Direct,* 1975

At life, all of us are rookies, and most of us can't hack nine innings.

> JOHN LEONARD
> *Private Lives in the Imperial City,*
> 1979

If life doesn't change you it's not worth living.

> RACHAEL MACKENZIE
> quoted in her obituary,
> the *New York Times,* March 30, 1980

No person has really seen life until he has talked with the ticket seller in a theater box office.

> quoted without attribution by
> H. V. PROCHNOW
> in *The Toastmaster's Treasure Chest,*
> 1979

Life is a Failure Opportunity.

> bumper sticker, cited by
> ELLEN GOODMAN
> in *Close to Home,* 1979

The one absolutely predictable thing in life is that circumstances will always change.

> ROBERT J. RINGER
> *Looking Out for Number 1,* 1977

In the small hours when the acrid stench of existence rises like sewer gas from everything created, the emptiness of life seems more terrible than its misery.

> CYRIL CONNOLLY

Life is like one of those modern kindergartens in which children are left to their own devices and work only at the subjects that arouse their interest.

> W. SOMERSET MAUGHAM
> *The Summing Up,* 1938

How you feel about yourself throughout the day is life itself.

> M. NEWMAN AND B. BERKOWITZ
> *How to Take Charge of Your Life,* 1977

Life's a pretty precious and wonderful thing. You can't sit down and let it lap around you. You have to plunge into it; you have to dive through it!

> KYLE CHRICHTON

Everyone lives by selling something.

> ROBERT LOUIS STEVENSON

Live all you can; it's a mistake not to. It doesn't much matter what you do in particular, so long as you have had your life. If you haven't had that what have you had? . . . What one loses one loses, make no mistake about that.

> STRETHER
> in Henry James' *The Ambassadors,* 1903

We break up life into little bits and fritter it away.
>   SENECA

Our life is like some vast lake that is slowly filling with the stream of our years. As the waters creep surely upward, the landmarks of the past are, one by one, submerged. But there shall always be memory to lift its head until the lake is overflowing.
>   ALEXANDRE BISSON

Life has meaning only in the struggle. Triumph or defeat is in the hands of the Gods. So let us celebrate the struggle.
>   Transcription of Swahili Warrior Song
>   featured in opening frame of the 1993 motion picture *Lorenzo's Oil*

One's real life is so often the life one does not lead.
>> OSCAR WILDE

Our life is what our thoughts make it.
>> MARCUS AURELIUS

Life is a series of experiences, each one of which makes us bigger, even though sometimes it is hard to realize this.
>> HENRY FORD

I'll tell you everything there is to know about life. What is, is, and what ain't, ain't.
>> est trainer STEWART EMERY
>> as quoted by Adelaide Bry in *Sixty Hours That Can Transform Your Life*, 1976

Life may be looked at as a continuing duet in which the individual and his or her environment each plays one of the two parts. With surprisingly few exceptions, there are no givens in life and any that are self-imposed or imposed from without may be challenged and changed. Life is not a final examination for which we may find the answers in the back of a book.

> RALPH CHARELL
> *How to Get the Upper Hand,* 1978

All life is an experiment. The more experiments you make the better.

> RALPH WALDO EMERSON

One should part from life as Odysseus parted from Nausicaa—blessing it rather than in love with it.

> FRIEDRICH NIETZSCHE
> *Beyond Good and Evil,* 1917

Life is like an ice cream cone: You have to learn how to lick it.

>   Charles Schulz

Life is short; live it up.

>   Nikita S. Khrushchev
>   the *New York Times Magazine*,
>   August 3, 1958

Life may be prodigious, enormous, morbidly distended, but never can it be quite full. I take "full" to mean full of energies, activities, deeds, emotions. Of course, it is always full of something, if only of inertia.

>   Rose Macauley
>   *A Casual Commentary*, 1926

People say that life is the thing, but I prefer reading.

>   Logan Pearsall Smith
>   *Myself*

Life is, soberly and accurately, the oddest affair; has in it the essence of reality. I used to feel this as a child—couldn't step across a puddle once, I remember, for thinking how strange—what am I? etc.

> VIRGINIA WOOLF
> *A Writer's Diary*, 1953

The great end of life is not knowledge but action.

> T. H. HUXLEY

Life's but a walking shadow, a poor player that struts and frets his hour upon the stage and then is heard no more. It is a tale, told by an idiot, full of sound and fury, signifying nothing.

> WILLIAM SHAKESPEARE
> *Macbeth*

Life is a tale told by an idiom, full of unsoundness and fury, signifying nonism.

> JAMES THURBER

That life is worth living is the most necessary of assumptions and, were it not assumed, the most impossible of conclusions.

> GEORGE SANTAYANA
> *The Life of Reason*, 1905

Life is a tragedy to those who feel, a comedy to those who think.

> HORACE WALPOLE

Life happens too fast for you ever to think about it. If you could just persuade people of this, but they insist on amassing information.

> KURT VONNEGUT, JR.

Man is not made to understand life, but to live it.

> GEORGE SANTAYANA

The best things in life are clean living, good works, and big sapphires. And not in that order.

> LAUREN BACALL
> quoted in a Fortunoff ad, 1981

I gave my life to learning how to live./ Now that I have organized it all .../ It is just about over.

> SANDRA HOCHMAN

Human life may be regarded as a succession of frontispieces. The way to be satisfied is never look back.

> WILLIAM HAZLITT
> *The Prose Album*, 1829

What we call reality is an agreement that people have arrived at to make life more livable.

> LOUISE NEVELSON
> quoted in *Newsweek* magazine,
> February 4, 1974

Life for the European is a career; for the American, it is a hazard.

> MARY MCCARTHY
> *On the Contrary*, 1961

Life's never quite interesting enough, somehow. You people who come to the movies know that.

> SHIRLEY BOOTH
> addressing the camera in the 1958
> motion picture *The Matchmaker.*

Life is one long process of getting tired.

> SAMUEL BUTLER
> *Notebooks*, 1913

Life is short. Work only pleases those who will never understand it. Idleness cannot degrade anybody. It differs greatly from laziness.

> AFRICAN CHIEFTAIN
> quoted in *Batouala*
> by Rene Maran, 1972

We're all in this together—by ourselves.

> LILY TOMLIN, on life
> quoted in the *New York Times*,
> September 12, 1976

As I grow to understand life less and less, I learn to live it more and more.

> JULES RENARD

We know life is futile. A man who considers that his life is of very wonderful importance is awfully close to a padded cell.

> CLARENCE DARROW
> lecture at the University
> of Chicago, 1929

It is a good thing that life is not as serious as it seems to a waiter.

> DON HEROLD

The first half of life is spent longing for the second, the second half in regretting the first.

> ALPHONSE KARR
> *Les Guepes, Juillet,* 1840

It is a funny thing about life; if you refuse to accept anything but the best, you very often get it.

> W. SOMERSET MAUGHAM
> *The Mixture as Before,* 1940

Life is like a game of cards. The hand that is dealt you represents determinism; the way you play it is free will.

> JAWAHARLAL NEHRU

What do you want a meaning for? Life is a desire, not a meaning. Desire is the theme of all life! It's what makes a rose want to be a rose and want to grow like that, and a rock want to contain itself and remain like that.

> CHARLIE CHAPLIN to a suicidal
> Claire Bloom in the 1952 motion
> picture *Limelight*

Our life is woven wind (*Notre vie est du vent tissu.*)

> JOUBERT
> *Pensées, Maximes et Essais,* Titre VII

The secret of getting the most out of life is never to expect too much out of it.

> O. A. BATTISTA
> in *Quotoons: A Speaker's Dictionary,*
> 1977

Life has meaning only if one barters it day by day for something other than itself.

ANTOINE DE SAINT-EXUPERY

If one wants to compare life to anything one must liken it to being blown through the Tube at fifty miles an hour.

VIRGINIA WOOLF

How do you go on the stage from 14 Ellwood Avenue, Quincy, Mass.? With no money, didn't know anybody on the stage, no looks, no nothing, five feet tall. How do you do that? That's the great philosophy of life I have learned—never face facts.

RUTH GORDON
quoted in the *Boston Herald American*, November 17, 1982

Life is a dream, and the dreams are dreams (*La vida es sueno, y los suenos, suenos son.*)

CALDERON DE LA BARCA

If you stop to think about it, life is like that big golf tournament. As soon as you get out of one hole, you start heading for another.

> HENNY YOUNGMAN

Life is nothing but a competition to be the criminal rather than the victim.

> BERTRAND RUSSELL
> as quoted by Alistair Cooke
> *Six Men*, 1977

Life itself is the proper binge.

> JULIA CHILD

[Life] is a rivulet, constantly passing away, and yet constantly coming on.

> ALEXANDER POPE

*Life is like a camel.
You can make it do anything
except back up.*

MARCELENE COX

In life you throw a ball. You hope it will reach a wall and bounce back so you can throw it again. You hope your friends will provide that wall.
>   PABLO PICASSO

Life is a drink of salt water, which seems to quench, but actually inflames.
>   ELIJAH GAON

In life, as in a football game, the principle to follow is: Hit the line hard.
>   THEODORE ROOSEVELT
>   *The Strenuous Life: The American Boy*, 1901

So live that you wouldn't be ashamed to sell the family parrot to the town gossip.
>   WILL ROGERS

Trust only movement. Life happens at the level of events, not of words. Trust movement.

> ALFRED ADLER

Try as much as possible to be wholly alive, with all your might, and when you laugh, laugh like hell and when you get angry, get good and angry. Try to be alive. You will be dead soon enough.

> WILLIAM SAROYAN

No matter what you do in life, you must do it with—it's a Jewish word—chutzpah. Energetically.

> RICHARD SIMMONS
> on *The Richard Simmons Show*,
> October 29, 1982

Showing up is eighty percent of life.

> WOODY ALLEN

All you need in life is clean underwear and a good haircut.
>
> BLAIR SOBOL

Yes! Life is a banquet, and most poor sons-of-bitches are starving to death! Live!
>
> JEROME LAWRENCE
> AND ROBERT E. LEE
> *Auntie Mame*, Act II, Scene vi, 1957

Every man's life is a fairy-tale written by God's fingers.
>
> HANS CHRISTIAN ANDERSEN

My father constantly told me to remember two things in life. Remember that things are not always what they seem. And never throw a change-up to a lousy hitter.
>
> an unnamed woman as quoted
> by JOHN D. SPOONER
> *Smart People*, 1979

The very meaninglessness of life forces a man to create his own meaning.

> STANLEY KUBRICK

Life n. 1. A burning up of questions. 2. A mere series of hungers and adverse forces, of petty contradictions which succeed or miscarry. 3. A costume grafted to a dead tree.

> excerpted from Artaud's *Dictionary*
> in *Antonin Artaud Anthology*,
> Jack Hirschman (ed.), 1965

One and one is two, right? That's what life is about. One and one is two.

> one bar stool drinker
> to another in a cartoon
> by ELDON DEDINI
> in *The New Yorker*, December 20, 1982

I don't understand life, but I think the key, if not the answer, to it is affirmation. We can't figure it out, any of us, but if we can embrace the mystery, it can be quite wonderful.

> HUME CRONYN
> quoted in the *New York Times Magazine*, December 26, 1982

Life is not long, and too much of it must not pass in idle deliberation how it shall be spent.

> DR. SAMUEL JOHNSON

Scientists are discovering at this very moment that to live as if to live and love were one is the only way of life for human beings, because, indeed, this is the way of life which the innate nature of man demands.

> ASHLEY MONTAGU

Life is a movie. Death is a photograph.

> SUSAN SONTAG

Life is just a bowl of cereal!
Life is just a bowl of M & Ms!
Life is just a bowl.

> captions to a three-panel cartoon
> by Roz Chast
> in *The New Yorker*, January 31, 1983

Life, however, is like war: The more you experience it, the more terrifying it becomes.

> Philip Caputo
> *The Horn of Africa*, 1980

Life and opulence are not compatible inasmuch as life is a quest while opulence is a status.

> Paolo Soleri

Life is a bus ride to the place of execution; all our squabbling and vying are about seats in the bus, and the ride is over before we know it.

> Eric Hoffer

The true meaning of life is to plant trees, under whose shade you do not expect to sit.

> NELSON HENDERSON
> also ascribed in slightly divergent
> form to Elton Trueblood

Life has a way of showering us with diamonds for nothing, having just exacted our blood for paste.

> PETER DE VRIES
> *Sauce for the Goose*, 1981

Hurried and worried until we're buried, and there's no curtain call,/ Life's a very funny proposition, after all.

> GEORGE M. COHAN
> *Life's Funny Propositions*, 1907

The essential wisdom of life is deflating. It is that the great task of life is transmission: the task of transmitting the essential tools and graces of life from our parents to our children. The two most important things to be transmitted are a mastery of logic and a capacity for sympathy.

> George F. Will
> *The Pursuit of Virtue and Other Tory Notions*, 1982

Life is a blister on top of a tumor, and a boil on top of that.

> Sholem Aleichem

Life shrinks or expands in proportion to one's courage.

> Anaïs Nin
> *The Diary of Anaïs Nin*, 1966

The key to life is how well you deal with Plan B.

> actress Marilu Henner
> quoted in *Esquire* magazine, January 1985

Life is a series of bad jokes, and death tops them all.
> A DINNER GUEST
> in television's *The Saint*

Life's jes pushin' side yo' troubles and lookin' for de light.
> AMERICAN PROVERB of unknown origin

The important thing [in life] is to learn a lesson every time you lose.
> JOHN MCENROE

Life is like an overlong drama through which we sit being nagged by the vague memories of having read the reviews.
> JOHN UPDIKE
> *The Coup*, 1978

Everything has been figured out except how to live.

> JEAN-PAUL SARTRE

There must be more to life than having everything.

> MAURICE SENDAK
> *Higglety Pigglety Pop!,* 1985

The difference between life and the movies is that a script has to make sense, and life doesn't.

> JOSEPH L. MANKIEWICZ

Let me tell you girls the three most important things I learned about life. Number one: Hold fast to your friends. Number two: There's no such thing as security. Number three: Don't go see *Ishtar.*

> SOPHIA
> in television's *The Golden Girls*

Life is a goddamned, stinking, treacherous game and nine hundred and ninety-nine men out of a thousand are bastards.

> THEODORE DREISER
> quoting an unnamed newspaper editor

All life is six to five against.

> DAMON RUNYON

Life does not begin at the moment of conception or the moment of birth. It begins when the kids leave home and the dog dies.

> quoted without attribution by
> R. BYRNE
> in *1,911 Best Things Anybody Ever Said*, 1988

Life being what it is, one dreams of revenge.
>> PAUL GAUGUIN

Life is an effort that deserves a better cause.
>> KARL KRAUS

In life, everything is one of two things—either everything is exactly as it seems or nothing is as it seems. The trick is to know which.
>> SUSAN PROFIT
>> *Wiseguy*

Life is a jest; and all things show it./ I thought so once; but now I know it.
>> JOHN GAY
>> *My Own Epitaph*

If a person is to get the meaning of life he must learn to like the facts about himself—ugly as they may seem to his sentimental vanity—before he can learn the truth behind the facts. And the truth is never ugly.

EUGENE O'NEILL

Life's a bitch and then you die.

BUMPER STICKER

Life is a pencil that death sharpens.

SOURCE OBSCURE

Life fascinates me, each moment as it comes along. I don't know that I have a philosophy, but I never do anything that doesn't entertain me.

JOHN HUSTON

The meaning of life is that it stops.

FRANZ KAFKA

It's like what one of those Middle West poets said: You've got to love life to have life, and you've got to have life to love life. It's what they call a vicious circle.

> THE STAGE MANAGER
> in Thornton Wilder's *Our Town*,
> Act II, 1938

Life is like a smooth stone; you rub it and rub it, and then you keep rubbing it and keep rubbing, and then when you think maybe you have a little something there, then you die.

> THE PARTY PHILOSOPHER
> in the 1986 motion picture *Always*

Life is something to do when you can't get to sleep.

> FRAN LEBOWITZ
> quoted by John Heilpern, *Observer*,
> January 21, 1979

A man's life is made up of a few intense moments, and the time spent in between is just packing and doesn't count.

> F. W. LISTER
> *The Wind That Blows*

Life to me is like boarding-house wallpaper. It takes a long time to get used to it, but when you finally do, you never notice that it's there. And then you hear the decorators are arriving.

> DEREK MARLOWE
> *A Dandy in Aspic,* 1966

Life is a cluster of disappointments made bearable by the challenges they establish.

> PETER VANSITTART
> *Paths From a White Horse,* 1985

Most people's lives—what are they but trails of debris, long long trails of debris with nothing to clean it all up but, finally, death.

> Mrs. Venable
> in Tennessee Williams'
> *Suddenly Last Summer*, 1958

Life is a mixed blessing which we vainly try to unmix.

> Mignon McLaughlin
> *The Complete Neurotic's Notebook*, 1981

Life is an unprofitable disturbance in the calm of nonexistence.

> Arthur Schopenhauer

Droll thing life is—that mysterious arrangement of merciless logic for a futile purpose. The most you can hope from it is some knowledge of yourself—that comes too late—a crop of inextinguishable regrets.

> Joseph Conrad
> *Heart of Darkness*, 1910

Life: A biological misadventure terminated on the shoulders of six strangers whose only objective is to make a hole in one with you.
>
> FRED ALLEN

The secret of life is to have a task, something you devote your whole life to, something you bring everything to, every minute of the day for your whole life. And the most important thing is—it must be something you cannot possibly do!
>
> sculptor HENRY MOORE
> quoted by Donald Hall
> in *Life Work*, 1993

Life leaps like a geyser for those who drill through inertia.
>
> ALEXIS CARREL

If life isn't hard, you're doing something wrong. . . . I learned a long time ago, if you don't do everything you can to help your lot in life and it fails, you'll just suffer endless regrets.

>   DAVID LETTERMAN
>   *Playboy* interview, 1993

Life is like laughing with a cracked rib.

>   JOHN-ROGER
>   AND PETER MCWILLIAMS
>   *Life 101*, 1991

Life is a romantic business. It is painting a picture, not doing a sum—but you have to make the romance, and it will come to the question how much fire you have in your belly.

>   OLIVER WENDELL HOLMES
>   letter to Oswald Ryan, March 8,
>   1911 as quoted in Biddle,
>   *Mr. Justice Holmes*

The ladder of life is full of splinters, but you never realize it until you begin to slide down.

> quoted without attribution by
> JACOB M. BRAUDE
> in *Source Book for Writers and Speakers*, 1968

So much of life is filled with the same dilemma: How to seem lusty and purposeful when less than nothing is going on.

> KURT VONNEGUT, JR.

The truth is, almost nothing in life is what it's cracked up to be—except perhaps the battle to get where you want to go.

> DONALD TRUMP
> *Trump: Surviving at the Top*, 1990

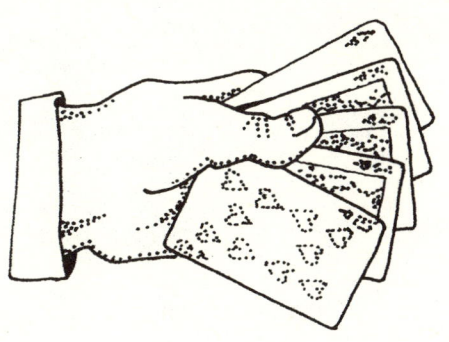

*In life, as in cards, two things go to produce success—
the first is chance; the second is cheating.*

GRANT ALLEN
The Episode of the Game of Poker

A life is a single letter in the alphabet. It can be meaningless. Or it can be part of a great meaning.

> JEWISH THEOLOGICAL SEMINARY
> ad featured in the *New York Times* and the *New York Herald*, September 5, 1956

How small it's all.

> JAMES JOYCE
> on life, in *Finnegan's Wake*, 1939

Life is one long struggle in the dark.

> LUCRETIUS
> *De rerum natura*

To burn always with this hard gem-like flame, to maintain this ecstasy, is success in life.

> WALTER PATER
> *The Renaissance*, 1877

Life is as tedious as a twice-told tale/Vexing the dull ear of a drowsy man.

> WILLIAM SHAKESPEARE
> *King John*, Act III

Life is an offensive, directed against the repetitious mechanism of the universe.

> ALFRED NORTH WHITEHEAD
> *Adventure of Ideas*, 1933

That it will never come again is what makes life so sweet.

> EMILY DICKINSON
> *Poem No. 1741*

For most men life is a search for the proper manila envelope in which to get themselves filed.

> CLIFTON FADIMAN
> quoted in *International Celebrity Register*, 1960

The art of living is the art of knowing how to believe lies.

> CESARE PAVESE
> *The Burning Brand*, 1961

Life is full of internal dramas, instantaneous and sensational, played to an audience of one.

> ANTHONY POWELL
> quoted in the *New York Times*,
> July 22, 1958

The greatest discovery of my generation is that a human being can alter his life by altering his attitude.

> WILLIAM JAMES

Life begins as a quest by the child for the man and ends as a journey by the man to rediscover the child.

> LAURENS VAN DER POST
> *The Lost World of the Kalahari*, 1958

One of the very nicest things about life is the way we must regularly stop whatever it is we are doing and devote our attention to eating.

> LUCIANO PAVAROTTI
> *My Own Story*

The most important things in life aren't things.

> quoted in the bulletin of the
> FIRST CHRISTIAN CHURCH
> Fairfield, Illinois

Enjoy the little things in life, for one day you may look back and realize they were the big things.

> ROBERT BRAULT
> in *National Enquirer*

A lifetime isn't nearly long enough to figure out what it's all about.

> DOUGLAS LARSEN
> United Feature Syndicate

Life isn't one straight line. Most of us have to be transplanted, like a tree, before we blossom.

                                                                                                      LOUISE NEVELSON

Would that life were like the shadow cast on a wall by a tree, but it is like the shadow of a bird in flight.

                                                                                                                THE *TALMUD*

What do we live for if it is not to make life less difficult for each other?

                                                                                                      GEORGE ELIOT

Life is a spiritual pickle preserving the body from decay.

                                                                                 AMBROSE BIERCE

Life is a little gleam of time between two eternities. . . . We emerge from the Inane; haste stormfully across the astonished Earth; then plunge again into the Inane.

                                                                                THOMAS CARLYLE

Life seems to be divided into two periods: In the first we indulge, in the second we preach.

> WILL DURANT

Life is a longish doze, interrupted by fits and starts of bewildered semi-alertness.

> CLIFTON FADIMAN

The best things in life never raise the white flag of surrender; they got to be taken by storm.

> O. A. BATTISTA
> in *Quotoons: A Speaker's Dictionary*, 1977

Life is the state which makes one unwilling to exchange what one has, no matter how grim, for the uncertainties of death, no matter how attractive.

> EUGENE E. BRUSSELL

Without discipline, there's no life at all.
> KATHARINE HEPBURN
> on *The Dick Cavett Show,*
> April 4, 1975

Most men make the voyage of life as if they carried sealed orders which they were not to open till they were fairly in mid-ocean.
> JAMES RUSSELL LOWELL
> "Dante," *Among My Books,* 1876

To enjoy life one should give up the lure of life.
> MOHANDAS K. GANDHI

Tell me not in mournful wish-wash/Life's a sort of sugared dish-wash.
> EZRA POUND
> *L'Homme Moyen Sensuel*

There are certain queer times and occasions in this strange mixed affair we call life when a man takes this whole universe for a vast practical joke, though the wit thereof he but dimly discerns, and more than suspects that the joke is at nobody's expense but his own.

> HERMAN MELVILLE
> *Moby Dick*, 1851

There is one reason why we cannot complain of life: it keeps no one against his will.

> SENECA
> *Epistulae ad Lucilium*

This is life: To have your A string snap and finish on three strings.

> HARRY EMERSON FOSDICK

What is life? Life is stepping down a step or sitting in a chair,/And it isn't there.

> Ogden Nash
> *You and Me and P. B. Shelley*, 1942

Life is pretty simple—you only need a comfortable bed and comfortable shoes, because you are in one or the other all of your life.

> quoted without attribution by
> H. V. Prochnow
> in *The Toastmaster's Treasure Chest*, 1979

Life is not so bad if you have plenty of luck, a good physique, and not too much imagination.

> Christopher Isherwood

Life is better than death, I believe, if only because it is less boring, and because it has fresh peaches in it.

> ALICE WALKER
> speech in San Francisco,
> March 16, 1982

Life is the lust of a lamp for the light that is dark till the dawn of the day when we die.

> ALGERNON CHARLES SWINBURNE
> *The Heptalogia*

If only one could live two lives: the first in which to make one's mistakes, which seem as if they have to be made; and the second in which to profit by them.

> D. H. LAWRENCE
> from *Collected Letters*, 1962

Isn't life a terrible thing, thank God?

> DYLAN THOMAS

"Live dangerously!" is advice we don't hear much any more since it turned out there isn't any other way.

> WILLIAM VAUGHN
> quoted in *Reader's Digest,*
> February 1960

Life is a succession of Paradises successively denied.

> SAMUEL BECKETT
> quoted in *New York Review of Books,*
> 1971

It is not the great expectations that make life interesting, but the little ones.

> MANUEL KOMROFF
> *Expect—and Live*

There is only one danger I find in life—you may take too many precautions.
>
> ALFRED ADLER
> quoted by Phyllis Bottome in
> *The Goal*, 1962

Life is the art of drawing without an eraser.
>
> JOHN CHRISTIAN

Too often man handles life as he does bad weather. He whiles away the time as he waits for it to stop.
>
> ALFRED POLGAR
> quoted in Oberndorf, *Germany*
> *Schwartzal der Bote*

It's a funny thing—you work all your life toward a certain goal and then somebody moves the posts on you.
>
> HERB CAEN
> in the *San Francisco Chronicle*

Human life is unsafe at any speed—and therein lies much of its fascination.

EDGAR ANSWEL MOWRER
Triumph and Turmoil, 1968

I don't know a better preparation for life than a love of poetry and a good digestion.

ZONA GALE

A life spent, however victoriously, in securing the necessaries of life is no more than an elaborate furnishing and decoration of apartments for the reception of a guest who is never to come.

ALFRED EDWARD HOUSMAN

To succeed in giving life some weight without making it too heavy, that is the whole problem.

JEAN ROSTAND

I look upon life as a party: One arrives long after it's started, and one's going to leave long before it's over, and it's as well, perhaps, not to try and be the life and soul of it, and not to try and take too much responsibility for it.

Robert Morley

Don't forget until too late that the business of life is not business, but living.

B. C. Forbes

Next to knowing when to seize an opportunity, the most important thing in life is to know when to forego an advantage.

Benjamin Disraeli

Life should be led like a cavalry charge.

Source Unknown
embroidered on a wall-hanging in
Allen Furniture Store in
Needham, Massachusetts, 1989

We cannot put off living until we are ready. The most salient characteristic of life is its coerciveness; it is always urgent, "here and now" without any possible postponement. Life is fired at us point blank.

ORTEGA Y GASSET

In great moments life seems neither right nor wrong, but something greater; it seems inevitable.

MARGARET SHERWOOD

Live as though life were earnest, and life will be so. What makes life weary is lack of motive.

AMERICAN PROVERB OF UNKNOWN ORIGIN

One need only remind oneself of all that we expect of life to see how very strange it is, and to arrive at the conclusion that man has found his way into it by mistake and does not really belong there.

> ITALO SVEVO
> *Confessions of Zeno,* 1923

The more science learns what life is, the more reluctant scientists are to define it.

> LEILA M. COYNE

The shortness of life can neither dissuade us from its pleasures nor console us for its pains.

> VAUVENARGUES
> *Reflections and Maxims,* 1746

Give me the luxuries of life and I will willingly do without the necessities.

> FRANK LLOYD WRIGHT

Life does not cease to be funny when people die any more than it ceases to be serious when people laugh.

>   GEORGE BERNARD SHAW

You should make a point of trying every experience in life once—except incest and folk-dancing.

>   ARNOLD BAX

Is life worth living? This is a question for an embryo, not for a man.

>   SAMUEL BUTLER

If you want my final opinion on the mystery of life and all that, I can give it to you in a nutshell. The universe is like a safe to which there is a combination. But the combination is locked up in the safe.

>   PETER DE VRIES

Life is so constructed that the event does not, can not, will not match the expectation.

> CHARLOTTE BRONTE
> *Villette*, 1853

On the rampage, and off the rampage—such is life!

> CHARLES DICKENS
> *Great Expectations*, 1861

Life is a battle, but it is so only in the sense that a game of chess is—there is no seriousness in it; it may be put an end to at any inconvenient moment by owning yourself beaten, with a careless "Ha-ha!" and sweeping your pieces into the box.

> THOMAS HARDY
> *The Hand of Ethelberta*, 1876

Human life is like a shadow, no sooner seemingly enjoyed than vanished.

> CHARLOTTE MCCARTHY

Life appears like a long shipwreck of which the debris are friendship, glory, and love. The shores of existence are strewn with them.

Madame de Stael

Life isn't bad for a first draft.

Joan Konner

I've learned, the hard way, that some poems don't rhyme, and some stories don't have a clear beginning, middle, and end. Life is about not knowing, having to change, taking the moment and making the best of it, without knowing what's going to happen next. Delicious ambiguity.

Gilda Radner

Life is like a great jazz riff. You sense the end the very moment you were wanting it to go on forever.

Sheila Ballantyne
Life on Earth, 1988

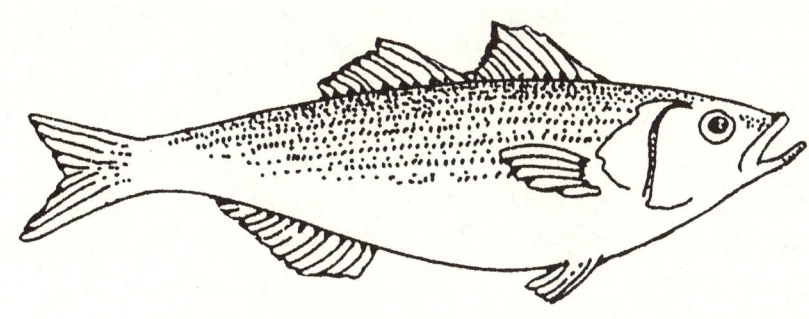

*Life is a fish that cannot be netted
by mood or doctrine,
but continually glides away
between sun and shadow.*

V. S. Pritchett

Life is a tragic mystery. We are pierced and driven by laws we only half understand, we find that the lesson we learn again and again is that of accepting heroic helplessness.

> FLORIDA SCOTT-MAXWELL
> *The Measure of My Days*, 1968

Man's life seems but an acting upon mysterious hints.

> HERMAN MELVILLE
> *Pierre*, 1852

It [life] began in mystery and it will end in mystery, but what a savage and beautiful country lies in between.

> DIANE ACKERMAN
> *A Natural History of the Senses*, 1990

Life seems to be a choice between two wrong answers.

> SHARYN MCCRUMB
> *If Ever I Return, Pretty Peggy-O*, 1990

Life cannot be captured in a few axioms. And that is just what I keep trying to do. But it won't work, for life is full of endless nuances and cannot be captured in just a few formulae.

> ETTY HILLESUM
> *An Interrupted Life*, 1983

If you wish to live, you must first attend your own funeral.

> KATHERINE MANSFIELD
> quoted in A. Alpen,
> *Katherine Mansfield*, 1954

The meaning of life is invented, not discovered.

> STEVEN M. CAHN

The universe is a blank slate and I believe there is no meaning to life. There are only valiant efforts to ward off the truth of an intrinsic void—individually and collectively—by coining a vocabulary of constructive behavior within the small unit of self, on toward the greater unit of a society.

GLORIA NAYLOR

Life is obstinate and clings closest where it is most hated.

MARY SHELLEY
Frankenstein, 1818

Recipe for Life. Directions: 1. Mix together chutzpah, love, dreams, political action, and fun; 2. Transfer into saucepan and add military budget (liquefied). Reduce by half over high heat, stirring constantly; 3. Yields health, education, and playgrounds for all the world's kids.

BEN AND JERRY
founders of Vermont's all-natural
ice cream empire

There's only one answer to the Mystery of Life. You do as much of it as you can.

> SPIKE MILLIGAN
> considered Britain's clown prince
> of comedy

To fight the dread fear that life has no meaning, we each seek to find it in mundane pursuits, such as the accumulation of wealth, or in everyday miracles like the birth of a child. And so we take part in the complex tapestry of life without ever seeing the grand design.

> BILLY BRAGG
> British musician/songwriter

The meaning of life is quite simple. Sit back, kick the cruise control into action, and enjoy the trip.

> TERRY TRACY, A/K/A TUBESTEAK
> famed Malibu surfer

I do not think there can be any general answer to the question, "What is the meaning of life?" Our individual lives have whatever meaning, or meanings, we succeed in giving them.

A. J. Ayer

Every time I come up with a philosophy of life, I find that my circumstances in life change and I have to come up with a new philosophy. Therefore, I have decided to drop the philosophy and to continue with my life.

Neil Simon

Life is a meaningless comma in the sentence of time.

Christ Garratt and Mick Kidd
The Essential Biff, 1982

Human life is only theater, and mostly cheap melodrama at that.

Malcolm Muggeridge
Tread Softly for You Tread on My Jokes, 1966

Life is a lease imposed upon the occupant without previous communication of the conditions in the contract.

> GUY DELAFOREST
> quoted in J. R. Solly, *Reflections on the Art of Life*, 1902

Death is life's answer to the question "Why?"

> GRAFFITI
> quoted in J. Green, *The Cynic's Lexicon*, 1984

Life is a tragedy when seen in close-up, but a comedy in long-shot.

> CHARLIE CHAPLIN
> *My Autobiography*, 1964

Life is an insane barrage of random madness and confusion, mixed with streams and semistreams of order and happiness. It's like a giant, bizarre cake made of gunpowder and sugar. Unlike a real cake with a real recipe, its ratio of ingredients can change constantly, making it almost impossible to accurately describe the taste at any instant.

STEVEN WRIGHT

Life is a tragedy—Hurrah!

GEORGES DUHAMEL
Scenes de la vie future, 1930

If a man hasn't discovered something that he will die for, he isn't fit to live.

MARTIN LUTHER KING, JR.
in a speech in Detroit, 1963

Life is short and we have not too much time for gladdening the lives of those who are travelling the dark road with us. Oh, be swift to love, make haste to be kind.

> HENRY FREDERIC AMIEL

Life is not lost by dying; life is lost minute by minute, day by dragging day, in all the thousand small uncaring ways.

> STEPHEN VINCENT BENET

To be on the wire is life. All the rest is waiting.

> KARL WALLENDA, later spoken
> by Roy Scheider
> in the 1979 motion picture
> *All That Jazz*

Life is a bubble on the stream.

> AMERICAN PROVERB
> quoted without attribution in
> Stevenson, *Home Book of Proverbs*,
> 1948

People hold on to life more than to anything else; it's really funny when you think of all the beautiful things there are in the world.

> Romain Gary
> *La Vie devant soi*, 1975

Life begins when you first realize how soon it ends.

> Alfred Armand Montapert

Life is a sickness which sleep relieves every sixteen hours, but it's only a palliative; death is the remedy.

> Chamfort
> *Maxims*, 1928

Life is a tough proposition, and the first hundred years are the hardest.

> Wilson Mizner

When first we fall in love, we feel that we know all there is to know about life, and perhaps we are right.

> Mignon McLaughlin
> *The Complete Neurotic's Notebook*,
> 1981

Life is a quarantine for Paradise.

> C. J. Weber
> *Demokritos*, V

And the days are not full enough/ And the nights are not full enough/ And life slips by like a field mouse/ Not shaking the grass.

> Ezra Pound
> Prologue to "Lustra" in *Personae*,
> 1926

The greatest pleasure in life is doing what people say you cannot do.

> Walter Bagehot

Ah, life and money both behave like loose quicksilver in a nest of cracks. When they're gone, you can't tell where or what the devil you did with them.

> Ray Collins
> in the 1942 motion picture
> *The Magnificent Ambersons*

We must make up for the threatened brevity of life by heightening the intensity of life.

> Joshua Liebman

You know what life is like? It's a great big parlour game of blind man's bluff, only everybody's blindfolded, creeping around, stumbling and bumping into one another—and then this Lord High Umpire slips off your blindfold and you see everything—your playmates still foolishly groping their way around, and the way into the conservatory, and where the refreshments are, and everything else.

> Anton Myrer
> *A Green Desire*, 1982

Life is a grand song. So let's start the music.

> RONALD REAGAN
> in his high school yearbook

We're living in a butcher shop. The fact that we die is the only comfort in the whole thing.

> LEONARD COHEN

The most important thing in life is not to capitalize on your gains. Any fool can do that. The really important thing is to profit from your losses. That requires intelligence, and it makes the difference between a man of sense and a fool.

> WILLIAM BOLITHO
> *Twelve Against the Gods,* 1957

Life is a game of errors; he who makes the fewest, wins.

> J. H. RHOADES
> *Jonathan's Apothogems,* 1942

The road through life is like the edge of a blade, with the nether-world on either side.

> THE SASSAOVER RABBI

Here is the test to find whether your mission on earth is finished: If you're alive it isn't.

> RICHARD BACH

The important thing about your lot in life is whether you use it for building or parking.

> quoted in *Dixiana Stampers Newsletter* as cited in *Reader's Digest*

Most men employ the earlier part of life to make the other part miserable.

> JEAN DE LA BRUYERE
> *Les Charactères*, 1865

Life is a test. It is only a test. If this were your actual life, you would have been given better instructions.

> a sign, referred to in a letter to the *Boston Globe*, January 10, 1991 from Rev. Diane Kessler, Director, Massachusetts Council of Churches

Life is so unlike theory.

> Anthony Trollope
> *Phineas Finn*, 1893

What is life? It is a flash of a firefly in the night. It is the breath of a buffalo in the wintertime. It is the little shadow which runs across the grass and loses itself in the sunset.

> last words of Crowfoot

When a person puts his best foot forward and gets it stepped on—that's life.

> Søren Kierkegaard

Life to me has been like one of those sections of the *autostrada* on the Italian Riviera on which there are lots of tunnels, some long, some short, with sunlit open spaces of varying lengths between them for which the darkness leaves one dazzled and unprepared.

> Eric Newby
> *A Traveler's Life*, 1982

Life is one long dirty trick.

> Thorne Smith

We begin to live when we have conceived life as tragedy.

> W. B. Yeats
> *Autobiography*, 1927

Life is not so important as the duties of life.

> John Randolph
> member of Congress in early nineteenth-century, quoted by W. C. Bruce in *John Randolph of Roanoke*, 1922

Life is just a series of trying to make up your mind.
> TIMOTHY FULLER
> *Reunion With Murder*, 1941

Look, I really don't want to wax philosophic, but I will say that if you're alive, you got to flap your arms and legs, you got to jump around a lot, you got to make a lot of noise, because life is the very opposition of death. And therefore, as I see it, if you're quiet, you're not living. You've got to be noisy, or at least your thoughts should be noisy and colorful and lively.
> MEL BROOKS

Life is a series of surprises, and would not be worth taking or keeping if it were not.
> RALPH WALDO EMERSON

There are only two or three human stories, and they go on repeating themselves as fiercely as if they had never happened before.

> WILLA CATHER
> *O Pioneers!*, 1913

Life, as it is called, is for most of us one long postponement.

> HENRY MILLER

Half of it is spent in night, and of the rest half is lost by childhood and old age. Work, grief, longing, and illness make up what remains.

> BHARTRIHARI, on life

It has begun to occur to me that life is a stage I'm going through.

> ELLEN GOODMAN
> *Close to Home*, 1979

Life is a preparation for the future, and the best preparation for the future is to live as if there were none.

> ELBERT HUBBARD
> in *The Philistine: A Periodical of Protest*, 1895–1915

The mystery of life is not a problem to be solved; it is a reality to be experienced.

> VAN DER LEEUW
> *The Conquest of Illusion*, 1928

A few years of youth and grace and then you fall flat on your face.

> WOLF BIERMANN

Don't hurry, don't worry. You're only here for a short visit. So be sure to stop and smell the flowers.

> WALTER HAGEN
> *New York Times*, May 22, 1977

Fortunately psychoanalysis is not the only way to resolve inner conflicts. Life itself still remains a very effective therapist.

> Karen Horney
> *Our Inner Conflicts*, 1945

There is not much comfort in life until one is old enough to have the courage of his cussedness.

> Don Herold

The final wisdom of life requires not the annulment of incongruity but the achievement of serenity within and above it.

> Reinhold Niebuhr

We do not know whether it is good to live or to die. Therefore, we should not take delight in living nor should we tremble at the thought of death. We should be equiminded towards both. This is the ideal.

> Mohandas K. Gandhi

*Life is a cup of tea; the more heartily we drink
the sooner we reach the dregs.*

JAMES M. BARRIE

The very commonplaces of life are components of its eternal mystery.

GERTRUDE ATHERTON

The art of living is more like that of wrestling than of dancing; the main thing is to stand firm and be ready for an unforeseen attack.

MARCUS AURELIUS

Life is too short to be long about the forms of it.

LAURENCE STERNE
A Sentimental Journey, 1832

The idea shared by many that life is a vale of tears is just as false as the idea shared by the great majority, the idea to which youth and health and riches incline you, that life is a place of entertainment.

LEO TOLSTOY

No one has learned the meaning of living until he has surrendered his ego to the service of his fellow men.

> WALTER BÈRAN WOLFE

Not everyone's life is what they make it. Some people's life is what other people make it.

> ALICE WALKER
> *You Can't Keep a Good Woman Down*, 1981

Life, like a dome of many-colored glass,/ Stains the white radiance of eternity.

> PERCY BYSSHE SHELLEY
> *Adonais*, 1821

Life is a feudal tenure for which nature exacts homage.

> WILLIAM DONALDSON
> *Sir Bartholomew Sapskull*

Life will taunt you with a million and one cheap things, but it will punish you if you accept anything less than the best it has to offer.

> O. A. BATTISTA,
> in *Quotoons: A Speaker's Dictionary*, 1977

Why shouldn't things be largely absurd, futile, and transitory? They are so, and we are so, and they and we go very well together.

> GEORGE SANTAYANA
> *Letters*, 1918

You have to relax in this hurry life. Rest while you're thinking. This will give you time to see straight. Then you will get the idea what life is.

> JOE FLYING BYE, South Dakota medicine man

Life is hard by the yard, but by the inch it's a cinch.

> AMERICAN PROVERB OF UNKNOWN ORIGIN

A philosopher once said to a fish, "The purpose of life is to reason and become wise." The fish answered, "The purpose of life is to swim and catch flies." The philosopher muttered "Poor fish." Back came a whisper, "Poor philosopher."

> Max Black

How many lives we live in one,/ And how much less than one, in all!

> Alice Cary
> *Life's Mysteries*

Life, then, is not Macbeth's "tale told by an idiot, full of sound and fury, signifying nothing." It is a grand orchestra in which discordant notes contribute to the total harmony.

> V.S. Seturaman, professor of English literature in Madras, India, quoted in D. Friend, *More Reflections on The Meaning of Life,* 1992

Life will give you what you ask of her if only you ask long enough and plainly enough.

> ELIZABETH NESBIT

"What makes life so difficult?"

"People."

> DEBORAH KERR AND CARY GRANT
> in the 1942 motion picture *An Affair to Remember*

Life is too short to stuff a mushroom.

> STORM JACKSON

I know of no way of going to the roots of life, except going to the roots of one's own life, secure in the confidence that the roots of all other lives are there, if you go deep enough.

> GAMALIEL BRADFORD
> *The Letters of Gamaliel Bradford*, 1934

There's always this about life: No man don't never get everything he sets out to get, but half the time he don't never find out he ain't got it.

SIDNEY HOWARD

Life is a hospital in which every patient is possessed by the desire to change his bed.

CHARLES BAUDELAIRE

Life is a child which must be rocked until it goes to sleep.

VOLTAIRE

Life, every now and then, behaves as if it had seen too many bad movies when everything fits too well—the beginning, the middle, and the end—from fade in to fade out.

HUMPHREY BOGART
commenting off camera
in the 1954 motion picture The Barefoot Contessa

The amount of satisfaction you get from life depends largely on your own ingenuity, self-sufficiency, and resourcefulness. People who wait around for life to supply their satisfaction usually find boredom instead.

> Dr. William Menninger

The secret of life is never to have an emotion that is unbecoming.

> Oscar Wilde

Life is like a lime. There are pips and juice and skin and pulp. You have to sample all of it, chew it, taste it, swallow it.

> Maxwell Fine, quoted by John D. Spooner in *Smart People*, 1979

Life for me ain't been no crystal stair.

> Langston Hughes

With food, as with life's two other basic necessities, clothing and shelter, the simplest fulfillment of basic requirements has never been enough. People at all times and in all cultures have pursued an instinct for embellishment.

> Mimi Sheraton
> quoted in the *New York Times*,
> May 25, 1983

Living is a form of not being sure, not knowing what's next or how. The moment you know how you begin to die a little.

> Agnes De Mille

Life's in parts, and some go together and some don't, and some incongruously don't, and the whole scheme is better left to itself.

> A Character in Joseph McElroy's
> *Women and Men*, 1987

Life is rather like a tin of sardines—we are all looking for the key.

> ALAN BENNETT
> *Beyond the Fringe*, 1963

Life is a sexually transmitted disease and there is a 100% mortality rate.

> R. D. LAING, as quoted by
> Peter Hilmore
> *Observer*, March 17, 1985

Life is perhaps best regarded as a bad dream between two awakenings.

> EUGENE O'NEILL
> *Marco Millions*, 1928

Life is an abnormal business.

> EUGENE IONESCO
> *Rhinoceros*, 1960

If life had a second edition, how I would correct the proofs.

> JOHN CLARE
> letter to a friend, quoted by J. W. Tibble and Anne Tibble in *John Clare: A Life*, 1932

The life of man is solitary, poor, nasty, brutish, and short.

> THOMAS HOBBES
> *Leviathan*, 1651

I look back on my life like a good day's work; it was done and I am satisfied with it. I was happy and contented, I knew nothing better and made the best out of what life offered. And life is what we make it, always has been, always will be.

> ANNA MARY "GRANDMA" MOSES
> *My Life's History*, 1951

Life is a matter about which we are lost if we reason either too much or too little.

> SAMUEL BUTLER

Life is the only riddle that we shrink from giving up.

> WILLIAM S. GILBERT

Life is a never-ending conflict between the impulse to find freshly available forms of gratification of the primary instincts and the constant tendency to revert to older forms even when these had proven less successful.

> SIGMUND FREUD

Life is like a mountain: After climbing up one side and sliding down the other, put up the sled.

> JOSH BILLINGS
> in *Josh Billings' Encyclopedia of Wit and Wisdom,* 1874

My advice to you is not to inquire why or whither, but just enjoy your ice cream while it's on your plate—that's my philosophy.

> THORNTON WILDER
> on life, in *The Skin of Our Teeth*, 1942

Life demands from you only the strength you possess. Only one feat is possible—not to have run away.

> DAG HAMMARSKJÖLD
> *Markings*, 1964

Life resembles the sword of Damocles; the sword is ever suspended.

> VOLTAIRE

In the game of life it's a good idea to have a few early losses, which relieves you of the pressure of trying to maintain an undefeated season.

> BILL VAUGHN
> in the *Kansas City Star*

The only thing certain in life is death and taxes.

> Daniel Defoe
> *History of the Devil,* 1726

Life is like a game of chess, in which there are an infinite number of complex moves possible. The choice is open, but the move contains within itself all future moves. One is free to choose, but what follows is the result of one's choice. From the consequences of one's actions there is never any escape.

> Shelley Smith
> *The Ballad of the Running Man,* 1961

The art of living lies not in eliminating but in growing with troubles.

> Bernard M. Baruch

There is no cure for birth and death save to enjoy the interval. The dark background which death supplied brings out the tender colours of life in all their purity.

> GEORGE SANTAYANA

Live your own life, for you die your own death. Make your life; don't copy it.

> AMERICAN PROVERB

Instead of looking at life as a narrowing funnel, we can see it ever widening to choose the things we want to do, to take the wisdoms we've learned and create something.

> LIZ CARPENTER

Don't be afraid your life will end; be afraid that it will never begin.

> GRACE HANSEN

Life isn't a matter of milestones but of moments.

Rose Fitzgerald Kennedy

Why couldn't God have built the universe and left it without anybody in it and just have had a ball with it? Well, that's not the idea of life. The idea of life is to give and receive, and if you didn't have anybody on earth to give to or receive from, then you'd have a very sad life.

Dizzy Gillespie

Life is not for everyone.

Michael O'Donoghue

Most people get a fair amount of fun out of their lives, but on balance life is suffering and only the very young or the very foolish imagine otherwise.

George Orwell
Shooting an Elephant, 1950

Human life begins on the other side of despair.
> JEAN-PAUL SARTRE
> *The Flies*, 1943

Life can then little else supply/ But a few good fucks and then we die.
> eighteenth-century British radical JOHN WILKES

I believe that every single event in life happens as an opportunity to choose love over fear.
> OPRAH WINFREY

Nothing seems so tragic to one who is old as the death of one who is young, and this alone proves that life is a good thing.
> ZOË AKINS

Let us so live that when we come to die even the undertaker will be sorry.

MARK TWAIN

Experience is a comb life gives you after you lose your hair.

JUDITH STERN

Life was meant to be lived. Curiosity must be kept alive. The fatal thing is the rejection. One must never, for whatever reason, turn his back on life.

ELEANOR ROOSEVELT

Life is composed of two parts: That which is past—a dream; and that which is to come—a wish.

ARAB PROVERB

But dost thou love life, then do not squander time, for that's the stuff life is made of.

BENJAMIN FRANKLIN

This is the only chance you will ever have on this earth with this exciting adventure called life. So why not plan it, and try to live it as richly, as happily as possible?

                        DALE CARNEGIE

"Tender teens; teachable twenties; tireless thirties; fiery forties; forceful fifties; serious sixties; sacred seventies; aching eighties; shortening breath; death; the sod; God." A good summary of life, isn't it?

                        JEAN RICH
                        Life

The tragedy of life is what dies inside a man while he lives.

                        ALBERT SCHWEITZER

Our grand business in life is not to see what lies dimly at a distance, but to do what lies clearly at hand.

                        THOMAS CARLYLE

We are here to add what we can to, not to get what we can from, life.

> SIR WILLIAM OSLER

Life is a battle in which we fall from the wounds we receive in running away.

> WILLIAM L. SULLIVAN

Life is a suck and a sell.

> WALT WHITMAN

I like living. I have sometimes been wildly, despairingly, acutely miserable, racked with sorrow, but through it all I still know quite certainly that just to be alive is a grand thing.

> AGATHA CHRISTIE

The fear of life is the favorite disease of the twentieth century.

> WILLIAM LYON PHELPS

Like gnats above a stagnant pool on a summer evening, man danced up and down without the faintest notion why.

> JOHN GALSWORTHY
> on life

To live is so startling it leaves little time for anything else.

> EMILY DICKINSON

Life to all of us is a narrow plank placed across a gulf, which yawns on either side, and if we were perpetually looking down into it we should fall.

> HALE WHITE

Not only is life a bitch, it has puppies.

> ADRIENNE E. GUSOFF

Life is choices: Always choose to do what you will remember ten years from now.

> RICHARD A. MORAN
> *Never Confuse a Memo With Reality*, 1993

Life is a moderately good play with a badly written third act.

> TRUMAN CAPOTE

Life is a cheap *table d'hôte* in a rather dirty restaurant, with time changing the plates before you've had enough of anything.

> THOMAS KETTLE

Life! Can't live with it, can't live without it.

> CYNTHIA NELMS

My whole life is a movie. It's just that there are no dissolves. I have to live every agonizing moment of it. My life needs editing.

> MORT SAHL

If life was fair, Elvis would be alive and all the impersonators would be dead.

JOHNNY CARSON

Life is just a vapor. You breathe in and what the heck.
>
> JERRY LEE LEWIS

Somebody told me life is a water wheel. It turns. The trick is to hold your nose when you're under it and not get dizzy when you're up.
>
> JAMES BALDWIN
> *Nobody Knows My Name,* 1961

Life's a tough proposition, and the first hundred years are the hardest.
>
> attributed to WILSON MIZNER

Life loves the liver of it. Life loves to be taken by the lapel and told "I am with you, kid. Let's go."
>
> educator MELVIN CHAPMAN,
> quoted by D. Riley
> in *My Soul Looks Back, 'Less I Forget,*
> 1993

Your whole life is on the other side of the glass. And there is nobody watching.

> ALAN BENNETT
> *The Old Country*

Life is a greedy pursuit of trifles.

> SHERWOOD ANDERSON

We all live in a house on fire, no fire department to call; no way out, just the upstairs window to look out of while the fire burns the house down with us trapped, locked in it.

> TENNESSEE WILLIAMS
> on life, in *The Milk Train Doesn't Stop Here Any More*, 1963

Life isn't a choice. Something comes up or it doesn't. A lot of choices choose you.

> KAREL REISZ
> British film director
> quoted in the *Daily Mail*, 1966

For myself I grow daily more convinced with a kind of inward delight amounting at times to ecstasy that the voyage of life is an episode of derisive insignificance.

> Malcolm Muggeridge

Life is a rock. And a hard place.

> Juli Duncan

Life is only a rather less inconsequent dream.
La vie est un songe un peu moins inconstant.

> Pascal
> *Pensées*

"What is the meaning of life?" is a stupid question. Life just exists.

> Jackie Mason
> comedian

The only real meaning in life can be found in a good man. And maybe Paris. Preferably the two together.

> MARILYN VOS SAVANT

Life is eating us up. We shall be fables presently. Keep cool: it will be all one a hundred years hence.

> RALPH WALDO EMERSON
> *Representative Men*, 1850

Since age two I've been waltzing up and down with the question of life's meaning. And I am obliged to report that the answer changes from week to week. When I know the answer, I know it absolutely; as soon as I know that I know it, I know that I know nothing.

> MAYA ANGELOU
> quoted by D. Friend, ed.
> *The Meaning of Life: Reflections in Words and Pictures on Why We Are Here*, 1991

Live as you will wish to have lived when you are dying.
> CHRISTIAN FURCHTEGOTT GELLERT

Life is a tragedy wherein we sit as spectators for awhile, and then act our part in it.
> JONATHAN SWIFT
> *Thoughts on Various Subjects*, 1706

In the end, all the best things to do in life usually end up in humiliation, arrest, or nudity.
> ROSEANNE BARR
> *My Lives*, 1994

The greatest use of a life is to spend it on something that will outlast it.
> WILLIAM JAMES

Life is little more than a loan shark: It exacts a very high rate of interest for the few pleasures it concedes.

LUIGI PIRANDELLO
The Pleasure of Honesty, 1917

Life is either always a tight-rope or a feather bed. Give me the tight-rope.

EDITH WHARTON

Life is like a cash register, in that every account, every thought, every deed, every sale, is registered and recorded.

BISHOP FULTON J. SHEEN

Life literally abounds in comedy if you just look around you.

MEL BROOKS

Life itself is a paradox: both meaningful and meaningless, important and insignificant, a joke and a yoke.

WES "SCOOP" NISKER

Life is God's joke on us. It's our mission to figure out the punchline.

> JOHN GUARRINE

Life is made up of constant calls to action, and we seldom have time for more than hastily contrived answers.

> LEARNED HAND

The common saying of life being a farce is true in every sense but the most important one, for it is a ridiculous tragedy, which is the worst kind of composition.

> JONATHAN SWIFT

All claims to discover the meaning or mystery of life rest on logical confusions.

> SIDNEY HOOK
> *Pragmatism and the Tragic Sense of Life,* 1974

Life is never so bad at its worst that it is impossible to live; it is never so good at its best that it is easy to live.

> GABRIEL HEATTER
> quoted in *Reader's Digest*, August 1954

Life is a like an egg in the hands of a child.

> ROUMANIAN PROVERB

We can have in life but one great experience at best, and the secret of life is to reproduce that experience as often as possible.

> OSCAR WILDE

Life is ten percent what you make it and ninety percent how you take it.

> quoted without attribution by E. MCKENZIE
> in *14,000 Quips & Quotes*, 1980

A man's life is dyed the color of his imagination.
>> SOURCE UNKNOWN

That daily life is really good one appreciates when one wakes from a horrible dream, or when one takes the first outing after a sickness. Why not realize it now?
>> WILLIAM LYON PHELPS
>> *Essays on Things,* 1930

A precipice in front of you, and wolves behind you; that is life.
>> LATIN PROVERB

What is the use of living, if it be not to strive for noble causes and to make this muddled world a better place to live in after we are gone?
>> WINSTON CHURCHILL

Life is intrinsically, well, boring and dangerous at the same time.
>> EDWARD GOREY

Actually it seems to me that one can hardly say anything either bad enough or good enough about life.

> C. S. LEWIS
> letter of February 8, 1956
> in *Letters of C. S. Lewis*

Life is made of ever so many partings welded together.

> CHARLES DICKENS

It is life near the bone where it is sweetest.

> HENRY DAVID THOREAU
> *Walden*, 1854

The trouble with life is that there are so many beautiful women, and so little time.

> JOHN BARRYMORE

We live in the midst of details that keep us running round in circles and never getting anywhere but tired, or that bring on nervous breakdowns and coronary thrombosis. The answer is not to take to the woods, but to find out what we really want to do and then cut out the details that fritter away what is most valuable in life. Live deep instead of fast. I think this is what Thoreau meant.

Henry Seidel Canby

Life is full of misery, loneliness, and suffering—and it's all over much too soon.

Woody Allen

Life is for most of us a continuous process of getting used to things we hadn't expected.

quoted without attribution
by E. Fuller
in *6200+ Wisecracks, Witty Remarks,
and Epigrams for All Occasions*, 1943

How goes a life? Something like the ocean building dead coral.
>> STANLEY MOSS

Why is life so tragic; so like a little strip of pavement over an abyss? I look down; I feel giddy; I wonder how I am ever to walk to the end.
>> VIRGINIA WOOLF

They that mistake life's accessories for life itself are like them that go too fast in a maze: their very haste confuses them.
>> SENECA

Do what you will, this life's a fiction,/ And is made up of contradiction.
>> WILLIAM BLAKE

Life is not a campaign of battle, but a laboratory where its possibilities for the enhancement of happiness and the realization of ideals are to be tested and observed.

> Randolph S. Bourne
> *The Experimental Life*

Life is a phenomenal thing, frontwards or backwards, however you swing.

> refrain from a pop tune in *Macho Camacho's Beat*, by Luis Rafael Sanchez, 1980

To be what we are, and to become what we are capable of becoming, is the only end of life.

> Robert Louis Stevenson

Life is a great big canvas, and you should throw all the paint on it you can.

> Danny Kaye

All life is a game of power. The object of the game is simple enough: to know what you want and get it.

> MICHAEL KORDA
> *Power in the Office,* 1976

The basic tension in life, I have come to think, is between changing and not changing. It's a conflict that can be felt every day in every area of our life.

> CHARLES SPEZZANO
> *What to Do Between Birth and Death,* 1992

Life is nothing but a dream, but few want to wake up.

> JEWISH PROVERB

What is the meaning of human life? To answer this question at all implied a religion. Is there any sense then, you ask, in putting it? I answer, the man who regards his own life and that of his fellow creatures as meaningless is not merely unfortunate but almost disqualified for life.

> ALBERT EINSTEIN
> *The World as I See It*, 1934

Our life resembles the Sibylline Books; the less there is left of it, the more precious it becomes.

> JOHANN WOLFGANG VON GOETHE

Life is a mission. Every other definition of life is false, and leads all who accept it astray. Religion, science, philosophy, though still at variance upon many points, all agree in this, that every existence is an aim.

> GIUSEPPE MAZZINI
> *Life and Writings*, 1890

Life is a fortress which neither you nor I know anything about.
NAPOLEON BONAPARTE

You know, your career is just your career. Your life is your life!
SISSY SPACEK

I would rather live in a world where my life is surrounded by mystery than live in a world so small that my mind could comprehend it.
HARRY EMERSON FOSDICK

A young student embarking on a career as a philosopher went into the mountains of the far Himalayas to speak to an elderly seer. He asked the sage, "Master, what is life?"

The sage closed his eyes in thought for a few moments, then replied, "Life is the smell of a fresh new rose."

"But master," said the young student, "in the Andes an elderly Inca told me that life was a sharp stone."

"That's his life," said the Himalayan sage.

SOURCE UNKNOWN

Because life is not a spectator sport.

ADVERTISING SLOGAN FOR
REEBOK ATHLETIC SHOES

It's a great thing to talk about or read in books, but when it comes to living it, life is pretty awful.

JEAN ANOUILH
Time Remembered, 1939

Measure thy life by loss instead of gain,/ Not by the wine drunk, but by the wine poured forth.

HARRIET KING
The Disciples

The whole secret of life is to be interested in one thing profoundly and in a thousand things well.

> HUGH WALPOLE
> quoted in *Reader's Digest*, November 1947

Life's a voyage that's homeward bound.

> HERMAN MELVILLE

Such is life.

> attributed to NED KELLY, his last words before being hanged on November 11, 1880
> as quoted in M. Clark, in *A History of Australia*, 1978

My life is caught in the lasso of existence.

> FRANTZ FANON
> *Black Skin, White Masks*, 1967

Your life feels different on you, once you greet death and understand your heart's position. You wear your life like a garment from the mission bundle sale ever after—lightly because you realize you paid nothing for it, cherishing because you know you won't ever come by such a bargain again.

> LOUISE ERDICH
> *Love Medicine,* 1984

There are two tragedies in life. One is not to get your heart's desire. The other is to get it.

> GEORGE BERNARD SHAW
> *Man and Superman,* 1903

Life is a practical joke.

> French chef PAUL BOCUSE
> *The Listener,* 1978

*Life is like drunkenness:
The pleasure passes away,
but the headache remains.*

PERSIAN PROVERB

Life is not worth living.

> Note left by murderer CHARLES WHITMAN, shot dead by police in 1966 after a rampage which left sixteen killed and thirty wounded.

We all live with the objective of being happy: our lives are all different and yet the same.

> ANNE FRANK

So many people go through life without a direction. They just go from stop to stop. It's like they're on a bus and the only time they get off is to piss.

> TODD RUNDGREN
> American rock musician

Life is not what you find, it's what you create.

> AMERICAN PROVERB OF UNKNOWN ORIGIN

Life being what it is in our world, the onset of death is often the first taste a man gets of freedom. At last the imagination can come into its own, and as a man yields to it his emotions take on a surprising depth and intensity.

> Isaac Rosenfelt
> *An Age of Enormity*, 1962

Is life so wretched? Isn't it rather your hands which are too small, your vision which is muddied? You are the one who must grow up.

> Dag Hammarskjöld
> *Markings*, 1964

Life is a constant battle between facing problems and finding their solutions, and success for most of us is to end life pretty much a draw.

> O. A. Battista
> in *Quotoons: A Speaker's Dictionary*, 1977

Life is divided up into the horrible and the miserable . . . the horrible would be, like, terminal cases, and blind people, crippled. I don't know how they get through life. It's amazing to me. And the miserable is everyone else.

> Woody Allen
> in the 1977 motion picture *Annie Hall*

Life is bliss; no person need suffer anymore.

> Maharishi Mahesh Yogi

WHAT IS LIFE? Life is a challenge, meet it. Life is a gift, accept it. Life is an adventure, dare it. Life is a sorrow, overcome it. Life is a tragedy, face it. Life is a duty, perform it. Life is a game, play it. Life is a mystery, unfold it. Life is a song, sing it. Life is an opportunity, take it. Life is a journey, complete it. Life is a promise, fulfill it. Life is a beauty, praise it. Life is a struggle, fight it. Life is a goal, achieve it. Life is a puzzle, solve it.

> Anonymous Epigram reprinted by Ann Landers on September 28, 1985

Life is a surgeon. It wounds, and administers no anesthetic. It cuts out almost the heart of us sometimes.

> Winifred Rhoades

Life is a negotiation.

> Wendy Wasserstein

In the deep of the night, lying on my back, I ask myself what life is and I see that I do not know; but I also see that it is a royal thing to be alive.

> Charles Ferdinand Ramuz
> *What is Man?*, 1948

Life shouldn't be printed on dollar bills.

CLIFFORD ODETS

Make your life a mission—not an intermission.

ARNOLD GLASGOW

The secret of living is to find a pivot, the pivot of a concept on which you can make your stand.

LUIGI PIRANDELLO

If you come to think of it, what a queer thing life is! So unlike anything else, don't you know, if you know what I mean.

P. G. WODEHOUSE
My Man Jeeves, 1919

I am certain that nothing in life is wasted—unless, of course, everything is.

MIGNON MCLAUGHLIN
The Complete Neurotic's Notebook, 1981

Those who have compared life to a dream were right.... We sleep when we are awake, and awake when sleeping.

> MICHEL DE MONTAIGNE
> *Essays*

The purpose of life is to fight maturity.

> RICHARD "DICK" WERTHIMER

I don't believe one grows older. I think that what happens early on in life is that at a certain age one stands still and stagnates.

> T. S. ELIOT
> on his seventieth birthday,
> quoted in the *New York Times*,
> September 21, 1958

Suicide is the sincerest form of criticism that life gets.

> WILFRED SHEED

Life itself is the real and most miraculous miracle of all. If anyone had never before seen a human hand and were suddenly presented for the first time with this strange and wonderful thing, what a miracle, what a magnificently shocking and inexplicable and mysterious thing it would be. In my plays I want to look at life—at the commonplace of existence—as if we had just turned a corner and run into it for the first time.

> CHRISTOPHER FRY
> in *Time* magazine, November 20, 1950

Life, looked at dispassionately, is such a hollow and stupid farce.

> MIKHAIL LERMONTOV
> *I Skuchno, i Grustno*

Listen, you son of a bitch, life isn't all a goddamn football game. You won't always get the girl! Life is rejection and pain and loss.

> FREDERICK EXLEY
> *A Fan's Notes*, 1977

There are two ways to slide easily through life: to believe everything or to doubt everything. Both ways save us from thinking.

> ALFRED KORZYBSKI
> *Manhood of Humanity*, 1950

A well-ordered life is like climbing a tower; the view halfway up is better than the view from the base, and it steadily becomes finer as the horizon expands.

> WILLIAM LYON PHELPS
> *Autobiography*, 1939

Life is a sentence man has to serve for being born.

> PEDRO CALDERÓN

Life at the greatest and best is but a froward child, that must be humored and coaxed a little to till it falls asleep, and then all the care is over.

> OLIVER GOLDSMITH
> *The Good-Natured Man*, 1768

The secret of life is not to do what one likes, but to try to like that which one has to do.

> DINAH MARIA MULOCK CRAIK

It is better to lead your own life, however bad, than to lead another's, however good.

> RALPH A. HABAS
> interpreting the *Bhagavad-Gita*

Life's under no obligation to give us what we expect. We take what we get and are thankful it's no worse than it is.

> MARGARET MITCHELL
> *Gone With the Wind*, 1936

Age and youth look upon life from the opposite ends of the telescope; to the one it is exceedingly long, to the other exceedingly short.

> HENRY WARD BEECHER

How impossible to describe life! How shameless of literature to poke its nose in everywhere! How can you use a pen to write about—blood!

> ANDREY SINYAVSKY
> *A Voice From the Chorus*, 1973

There is no meaning to life except the meaning man gives his life by the unfolding of his powers, by living productively.

> ERICH FROMM

There are but three events in a man's life: birth, life and death. He is not conscious of being born, he dies in pain, and he forgets to live.

> JEAN DE LA BRUYERE
> *Charactères*, 1688

Life is meant to be lived. The miser who hoards it only cheats himself.

> GERI TROTTA

I look on life as a progressive game that is being played for some purpose, probably for self-entertainment. I hold that there is no evidence to show that this game, as played here, is planned to solve anything.

> THEODORE DREISER
> letter to George Douglas,
> January 26, 1935

Life consists in penetrating the unknown, and fashioning our actions in accord with the new knowledge thus acquired.

> LEO TOLSTOY

Life is a fatal adventure. It can only have one end. So why not make it as far ranging and free as possible.

> ALEXANDER ELIOT
> in the *New York Post*,
> November 28, 1962

Most people's lives aren't complex—they're just complicated.

> RUST HILLS
> American journalist
> *Esquire* magazine, 1970

One's life should be a self-created contradiction of the fact that life is basically absurd.

> DAVID MADDEN
> British novelist
> in *Contemporary Novelists*, 1976

Life's cup is nectar at the brink,/ Midway a palatable drink,/ And wormwood at the bottom.

> JASON SMITH
> *Chigwell Revisited*

Life is like backgammon—half skill and half luck.

> OLIVER WENDELL HOLMES, JR.

Life is really a game and you must treat it as a game. . . . Life stinks, but that doesn't mean you don't enjoy it.

> DUSTIN HOFFMAN
> *Playboy* interview, 1975

The goal of all life is death.

> SIGMUND FREUD

It is the essence of life that it exists for its own sake.

> ALFRED NORTH WHITEHEAD
> *Nature and Life*, 1934

I compare human life to a large mansion of many apartments, two of which I can only describe, the doors of the rest being as yet shut upon me.

> JOHN KEATS
> letter to John Hamilton Reynolds,
> May 3, 1818

Life is trouble. Only death is not. To be alive is to undo your belt and look for trouble.

> ANTHONY QUINN
> in the 1964 motion picture *Zorba the Greek*

Life is like a butterfly. You can chase it, or you can let it come to you.

> RUTH BROWN

We must not try to manipulate life; rather we must find out what life demands of us, and train ourselves to fulfill these demands. It is a long and humble business.

> PHYLLIS BOTTOME
> quoted in *Reader's Digest*
> November 1943

Life is half spent before we know what it is.

> GEORGE HERBERT
> *Outlandish Proverbs*, 1640

Life is made up of small comings and goings, and for everything that we take with us, there is something that we leave behind.
> from the 1971 motion picture
> *Summer of '42*

Even without wars, life is dangerous.
> ANNE SEXTON
> *The Death Notebooks*, 1974

Human life is like a poem: It has a beginning and an end, but does not comprise a whole.
> JOHANN WOLFGANG VON GOETHE
> *Faust*, 1819–21

Life's a rash, and then there's death and the itching's over.
> CYNTHIA KRAMAN

Life is only heaven's mockery of earth.
> ALEKSANDR SERGEEVOCH PUSHKIN
> *The Bronze Horseman*

To live is to suffer; to survive is to find some meaning in the suffering.

> Roberta Flack
> quoted in *Essence* magazine,
> February 1989

Life is too serious to be taken seriously.

> G. L. Walton
> *Peg Alone*, 1915,
> later used without attribution by
> comedienne Carol Burnett

Life is like a dogsled team. If you ain't the lead dog, the scenery never changes.

> Lewis Grizzard
> quoted in *People* magazine
> April 4, 1994

We learn the rope of life by untying its knots.

> JEAN TOOMER
> *Definitions and Aphorisms*, 1931

We go up the hill of life like a boy with his sled after him, and go down it like a boy with his sled under him.

> quoted without attribution by
> HENRY HUPFELD
> in *Wit and Wisdom*, 1876

Life is the best party I've ever been invited to.

> ARLENE FRANCIS
> *A Memoir by Arlene Francis*, 1978

There are only two ways to live your life. One is as though nothing is a miracle. The other is as though everything were a miracle.

> ALBERT EINSTEIN

Life does not agree with philosophy: there is no happiness that is not idleness, and only what is useless is pleasurable.
>> ANTON CHEKHOV

Life is a total war. No one has the right to be a conscientious objector.
>> PARISIAN BISTRO OWNER to former gendarme in 1963 motion picture *Irma La Douce*

Life may begin at forty, but so does rheumatism.
>> HERBERT V. PROCHNOW

The lesson of life is to believe what the years and centuries say against the hours.
>> RALPH WALDO EMERSON

Life would be infinitely happier if we could only begin at the age of eighty and gradually approach eighteen.

> Mark Twain

We do not weave the web of life: We are merely a strand in it.

> Chief Seattle

I think games are significant in people's lives because in a game everything is clearly defined. You've got the rules and a given period of time in which to play; you've got boundaries and a beginning and an end. And whether you win, lose, or draw, at least something is sure. But life ain't like that at all. So I think people invent and play games in order to kid themselves, at least for a time, into thinking that life is a game; in order to forget that at the end of life there is nothing but a big blank wall.

> James Jones
> quoted in *Writers at Work*, 3rd Series, 1967

Life is a search for truth, and there is no truth.

> CHINESE PROVERB

Whether you have been knocked down, or are on the ropes, always remember that life is ninety-nine rounds.

> Attributed to an unnamed friend of former president RICHARD NIXON in *People* magazine, May 9, 1994

Life is a shit sandwich, but if you've got enough bread, you don't taste the shit.

> JONATHAN WINTERS

Life would be one delightful slide if we did not have to drag our sleds back up the hill.

> quoted without attribution in *Grit* magazine

In the great game of human life, one begins by being a dupe and ends by being a rogue.

> Voltaire

Life is ten per cent carrot and ninety percent stick.

> ex-cop Mitch Tobin
> in Donald Westlake's *Wax Apple*,
> 1970

The prime of life: a few slippery years between too-young and too-old.

> Mignon McLaughlin
> *The Complete Neurotic's Notebook*, 1981

The ups and downs of life that one lives through and survives are the only things that give dimension and color and flavor to life.

> Dr. Galen Starr Ross, then-President of Capitol College of Oratory and Music

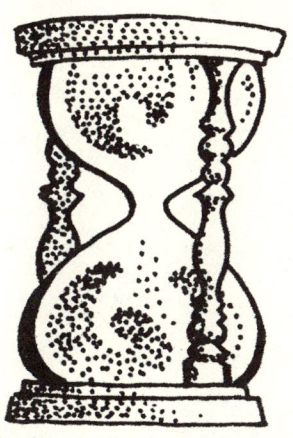

Like sands through the hourglass, so are the days of our lives.

OPENING THEME OF DAYTIME
SOAP OPERA *Days of Our Lives*

All of life is basically a magnified version of high school.

> MARJORIE WILLIAMS
> in *Vanity Fair*, July 1994

I've looked at life from both sides now/ From up and down, and still somehow/ It's life's illusions I recall/ I really don't know life at all.

> JONI MITCHELL
> from the 1969 song "Both Sides Now"

The first thing in life is to assume a pose. What the second one is, no one has yet discovered.

> OSCAR WILDE

Now at last I have come to see what life is/ Nothing is ever ended, everything only begun,/ And the brave victories that seem so splendid/ Are never really won.

> SARA TEASDALE
> *At Midnight*

To live remains an art which everyone must learn and which no one can teach.

HAVELOCK ELLIS

I have never given very deep thought to a philosophy of life, though I have a few ideas that I think are useful to me. One is that you do whatever comes your way to do as well as you can, and another is that you think as little as possible about yourself and as much as possible about other people and about things that are interesting. The third is that you get more joy out of giving joy to others.

ELEANOR ROOSEVELT
McCall's magazine, September 1957

Life is as uncertain as a grapefruit's squirt.

quoted without attribution by
E. MCKENZIE
in 14,000 Quips & Quotes, 1980

Life is merely the messy consequence of "a lack of antiseptic precaution on the part of the cosmos."

> EDDINGTON, quoted by John Leonard
> in *Private Lives in the Imperial City*, 1979

Life is made up of marble and mud.

> NATHANIEL HAWTHORNE
> *The House of the Seven Gables*, 1851

Life is like going through a girl's room; a rambling mess as far as you can see.

> American twelve-year-old
> LAURIE FAURE
> quoted in *Journey: Prose by Children of the English-speaking world*, collected by Richard Lewis

Life is always at some turning point.
> Irwin Edman, quoted by C. Frankel
> in *The Uses of Philosophy*, 1955

Forgive, O Lord, my little jokes on Thee/ And I'll forgive Thy great big one on me.
> Robert Frost, on life

Life consists not simply in what heredity and environment do to us but in what we make out of what they do to us.
> Harry Emerson Fosdick

Well, I have found life an enjoyable, enchanting, active, and sometimes a terrifying experience, and I've enjoyed it completely. A lament in one ear, maybe, but always a song in the other. And to me life is simply an invitation to live.
> Sean O'Casey
> *Wisdom*, J. Nelson ed.

The main obligation is to amuse yourself.

> S. J. Perelman, on life

To be sure, I occasionally pretended to take life seriously. But very soon the frivolity of seriousness struck me. . . .

> Jean-Baptiste Clamence
> in Albert Camus' *The Fall*, 1956

Reality is something you rise above.

> Liza Minnelli

We are grown stiff with the ramrod of convention down our backs. We pass on; and some day we come, at the end of a very dull life, to reflect that our romance has been a pallid thing of a marriage or two, a satin rosette kept in a safe-deposit drawer, and a life-long feud with a steam radiator.

> O. Henry

Life is like a dusty corridor, I say,/ Shut at both ends.
>
> Roy Campbell
> *The Flaming Terrapin*, 1924

The hardest thing to learn in life is which bridge to cross and which to burn.
>
> David Russell

A life spent making mistakes is not only more honorable but more useful than a life spent doing nothing.
>
> George Bernard Shaw

Old and young, we are all on our last cruise.
>
> Robert Louis Stevenson,
> on life, in *Crabbed Age and Youth*

It is so hard for us little human beings to accept this deal that we get. It's really crazy, isn't it? We get to live, then we have to die. What we put into every moment is all we have. . . . What spirit human beings have! It is a pretty cheesy deal—all the pleasures of life, and then death.

> GILDA RADNER
> *It's Always Something*, 1989

To enter life by way of the vagina is as good a way as any.

> HENRY MILLER

Life is a terrible disease—cured only by death.

> HAI GAON
> *Musar Haskel*

"Life is a thief," Sebastian always said, "Life steals everything."

> KATHARINE HEPBURN TO
> MONTGOMERY CLIFT, referring
> to her late son
> in the 1959 motion picture
> *Suddenly, Last Summer*

Life's a pudding full of plums.

> WILLIAM S. GILBERT
> *The Gondoliers*, 1889

Life is a rose that withers in the iron fist of dogma.

> GEORGE MOORE
> *Epigrams of George Moore*

We occasionally meet with one possessing sufficient philosophy to look upon life as a pilgrimmage.

> from *Colonel Crockett's Exploits and
> Adventures in Texas,* of uncertain
> authorship, 1836

The years don't last as long as you think they are going to.
> WALTER LIPPMAN, at age 80

Life is a traveller who lets his suitcase drag behind him to cover his tracks.
> LOUIS ARAGON
> French playwright
> *Les Voyageurs de l'imperiale*

The only time you live fully is from thirty to sixty.
> WILLIAM HERVEY ALLEN

We are all in the gutter, but some of us are looking up at the stars.
> OSCAR WILDE

Life was a funny thing that happened to me on the way to the grave.
> QUENTIN CRISP
> *The Naked Civil Servant*, 1968

Life is a game whose rules each of us invents for himself. No one knows the rules. Reality is continually unreal, but is also continually real. What we do is invent something which also exists.

ALAIN ROBBE-GRILLET
in the *Guardian*, 1967

1. You can't win.
2. You can't break even.
3. You can't even quit the game.

Ginsberg's Theorem of life,
quoted by Arthur Bloch
in *Murphy's Law*, 1979

Existence is no more than the precarious attainment of relevance in an intensely mobile flux of past, present, and future.

SUSAN SONTAG
Styles of Radical Will, 1969

Our life is a book that writes itself alone. We are characters in a novel who don't always understand very well what the author wants.

> JULIEN GREEN
> *Journal*

Life is an obscene farce, never a tragedy! Pain's the first principal on which the universe is built. Terror is the second. Lust is the third, followed by madness, followed by death.

> FRANK YERBY
> *My Brother*, 1967

It happens in life, as in grammar, that the exceptions outnumber the rules.

> RÉMY DE GOURMANT

Life is God's novel so let him write it.

> ISAAC BASHEVIS SINGER

Three things in human life are important: the first is to be kind. The second is to be kind. And the third is to be kind.

>   HENRY JAMES

Expecting life to treat you well because you are a good person is like expecting an angry bull not to charge because you are a vegetarian.

>   SHARI R. BARR

There are men here and there to whom the whole of life is like an after-dinner hour with a cigar: easy, pleasant, empty, perhaps enlivened by some fable of strife to be forgotten before the end is told.

>   JOSEPH CONRAD
>   *Lord Jim*, 1900

To live is to climb the Andes: The more one climbs, the steeper become the precipices.

>   EUGENIA MARIA DE HOSTOS
>   *Obras*, 1939–54

The rule of my life is to make business a pleasure, and pleasure my business.

> AARON BURR

The only way to live is as though there were an answer to every problem—although there isn't.

> ANDREW A. ROONEY
> *And More by Andy Rooney*, 1982

Life is infinitely stranger than anything which the mind of man could invent.

> SHERLOCK HOLMES

Life is a one-way street. No matter how many detours you take, none of them leads back. And once you know and accept that, life becomes much simpler. Because then you know you must do the best you can with what you have and what you have become.

> ISABEL MOORE
> quoted in *Reader's Digest*, October 1942

A man has lived to no purpose unless he has either built a house, begotten a son, or written a book.

> ITALIAN PROVERB

Anything you want in life is available, even free, if you have enough appetite for it.

> CHARLES GAINES
> *A Family Place*, 1994

To change one's life: Start immediately. Do it flambuoyantly. No exceptions.

> WILLIAM JAMES

Life is brutal, arbitrary, disconnected, full of inexplicable, illogical and contradictory disasters which can only be classified under the heading "Other news in brief."

> GUY DE MAUPASSANT
> *Pierre et Jean*, 1887

The wisdom of life consists in the eliminating of non-essentials.
LIN YUTANG

"So live as if you were living already for the second time and as if you had acted the first time as wrongly as you are about to act now!" It seems to me that there is nothing that would stimulate a man's sense of responsibleness more than this maxim, which invites him to imagine first that the present is past and, second, that the past may yet be changed and amended.
VIKTOR E. FRANKL

Life is a mighty maze, but not without a plan.
ALEXANDER POPE

Life is made up, not of great sacrifices or duties, but of little things, in which smiles and kindnesses, and small obligations, given habitually, are what win and preserve the heart and secure comfort.
SIR H. DAVY

Our lives are largely made up of things we do not have.

> CHARLES DUDLEY WARNER
> *A Little Journey*, 1899

It is impossible to cheat life. There are no answers to the problems of life in the back of the book.

> SØREN KIERKEGAARD

If it were possible to talk to the unborn, one could never explain to them how it feels to be alive, for life is washed in the speechless real.

> JACQUES BARZUN
> *The House of Intellect*, 1959

If you want to give God a good laugh, tell him your plans.

> YIDDISH FOLK SAYING

Men, for the sake of getting a living, forget to live.

> MARGARET FULLER
> *Summer on the Lakes*, 1844

Life is a maze in which we take the wrong turning before we have learnt to walk.

> CYRIL CONNOLLY
> *The Unquiet Grave*, 1945

If by the time we're sixty we haven't learned what a knot of paradox and contradiction life is . . . we haven't grown old to much purpose.

> JOHN COWPER POWYS
> *The Art of Growing Old*, 1944

In spite of everything, life is good.

> HENDRIK VAN LOON

Our whole life is but a greater and longer childhood.

> Thomas Fuller
> *Gnomologia*, 1732

Life is a child playing round your feet, a tool you hold firmly in your grip, a bench you sit down upon in the evening, in your garden.

> Jean Anouilh
> *Antigone*, 1946

Life is difficult.

> Famous first sentence of
> M. Scott Peck's
> *The Road Less Traveled*, 1978

The great business of life is to be, to do, to do without, and to depart.

> John Morley
> *Address to Aphorisms*, 1887

There is no incidental music to the dramas of real life.

> SAX ROHMER
> *Insidious Dr. Fu Manchu*, 1913

Life is a naked goddess and we must come to her unclothed and unashamed. A naked mind has no pockets.

> NORMAN LINDSAY
> *Creative Effort*, 1920

Life is the childhood of our immortality.

> JOHANN WOLFGANG VON GOETHE

Remember that life is neither pain nor pleasure; it is serious business, to be entered upon with courage and in a spirit of self-sacrifice.

> ALEXIS DE TOCQUEVILLE

To make good use of life, one should have in youth the experience of advanced years, and in old age the vigor of youth.
> STANISLAS I

Life is constantly providing us with new funds, new resources even when we are reduced to immobility. In life's ledger there is no such thing as frozen assets.
> HENRY MILLER
> *Quiet Days in Clichy*, 1956

Life grows as it is spent.
> ARDIS WHITMAN
> quoted in *Reader's Digest*, April 1972

To get all there is out of living we must employ our time wisely: never being in too much of a hurry to stop and sip life, but never losing our sense of the enormous value of a minute.
> ROBERT RAWLS UPDEGRAFF

The ring is the very essence of life itself.

> LUIS MIGUEL DOMINGUIN
> Spanish bullfighter, 1959

One of life's compensations is that there is always something ahead.

> GERTRUDE ATHERTON

Wisdom, science, power, learning—all these are as blind and impotent before the great problem of life as ignorance and weakness.

> JOSIAH GILBERT HOLLAND
> *Arthur Bonnicastle*, 1901

Study as if you were to live forever. Live as if you were to die tomorrow.

> ISIDORE OF SEVILLE

Life is like a train. You expect delays from time to time. But not a derailment.

WILLIE STARGELL
baseball player, 1976

It seems to me you can be awfully happy in this life if you stand aside and watch and mind your own business and let other people do as they like about damaging themselves and one another. You go on kidding yourself that you're impartial and tolerant and all that, then all of a sudden you realize you're dead, and you've never been alive at all.

MARY STEWART
This Rough Magic, 1964

Most of us would enjoy living the simple life if the way back to it weren't so complicated.

ANNA HERBERT

Life is a series of little deaths out of which life always returns.

CHARLES FEIDELSON, JR.

I am convinced that there is no man that knows life well, and remembers all the incidents of his past existence, who would accept it again.

EDWARD CAMPBELL

Life has its ups and downs.

JOSEPH S. JONES
Life of Jefferson S. Batkins, 1871

Anyone who has survived childhood has enough information about life to last him the rest of his days.

FLANNERY O'CONNOR

Life is like a blind date. Sometimes you just have to have a little faith!

AN UNNAMED 23-YEAR-OLD
quoted in H. Jackson Brown, *Live and Learn and Pass It On,* 1991

Life is a flame whose splendor hides its base.

> GEORGE TUFTS

Life is worth being lived, but not being discussed all the time.

> French actress ISABELLE ADJANI,
> quoted in *Time* magazine, 1979

It is the essence of life that it exists for its own sake.

> ALFRED NORTH WHITEHEAD
> *Nature and Life*

Life is simply an accumulation of all the forces that resist death.

> HEATHCOTE WILLIAMS
> British playwright
> *The Immortalist*

Unless you stake your life, life will not be won.

> WERNER HEISENBERG
> German scientist
> *Physics and Beyond,* 1971

Let us confess it—the human situation is always desperate.

> LEWIS MUMFORD
> *In the Name of Sanity,* 1954

Life is a contact sport.

> KEN KRAGEN
> *Life is a Contact Sport,* 1994

Our daily life is a bad serial by which we let ourselves be bewitched.

> MICHEL BUTOR
> French writer
> *Repertoire II,* 1960

There is no end. There is no beginning. There is only the infinite passion of life.

> FEDERICO FELLINI

He who asks of life nothing but the improvement of his own nature is less liable than anyone else to miss and waste life.

> HENRI FREDERIC AMIEL

Life, friends, is boring. We must not say so.

> JOHN BERRYMAN
> poet
> *Dream Songs*, 1969

To contemplate human life for forty years is the same as contemplating it for ten thousand. In ten thousand, what more will you see?

> MARCUS AURELIUS
> *Meditations*, VII

Continue on the yam level and life will be sweet.

> RALPH ELLISON
> *Going to the Territory*, 1986

It has always been difficult for man to realize that his life is all an art. It has been more difficult to conceive it so than to act it so.

> HAVELOCK ELLIS
> *The Dance of Life*, 1923

Life consists in wanting something. When a man is satisfied he is as good as dead.

> AUTHOR UNKNOWN

There is a moment in this repast we call life where we reach saturation point; after that, it needs only a drop more to make the cup of disgust run over.

> CHARLES AUGUSTIN SAINTE-BEUVRE
> *Causeries du Lundi*, 1894

Life's challenges are not supposed to paralyze you, they're supposed to help you discover who you are.

> BERNICE JOHNSON REAGON

If you can spend a perfectly useless afternoon in a perfectly useless manner, you have learned how to live.

> LIN YUTANG

Life is a wreath of curling smoke, and men spit out their bitter last days as one spits out the butt of a cigar.

> JOSHUA STEINBERG
> Hebrew author

The obstinate insisting that Tweedledum is not Tweedledee is the bone and marrow of life.

> WILLIAM JAMES

Life is a bucket of shit with both handles on the inside.
SOURCE OBSCURE

Life itself is a bubble and a skepticism, and a sleep within a sleep.
RALPH WALDO EMERSON

In real life it only takes one to make a quarrel.
OGDEN NASH
The Ogden Nash Pocket Book

A friend of Ivan Turgenev once wrote to him, "It seems to me that to put oneself in the second place is the whole significance of life." To this the great Russian author replied: "It seems to me to discover what to put before oneself in the first place is the whole problem of life."
ROBERT E. LUCCOCK

Life is not a dress rehearsal.

> Source Obscure

Life is a frontier. Though we know what is behind us, we do not know what is ahead of us. Our capacity and willingness to hazard our lives on something as we move out into the unknown, ultimately determines the tenor of our existence.

> Rabbi Solomon Roodman

Life is a cabaret, ol' chum.

> Title song from the Broadway musical *Cabaret*

Anyone can carry his burden, however heavy, until nightfall. Anyone can do his work, however hard, for one day. Anyone can live sweetly, patiently, lovingly, purely, till the sun goes down. And this is all that life ever really means.

> F.R.L. Newbery

Life hardens what is soft within us and softens what is hard.
> Dr. Joseph Fort Newton
> quoted in *Reader's Digest*, March 1956

Life moves pretty fast; you don't stop and look around every once in a while, you could miss it.
> Matthew Broderick
> in the 1986 motion picture *Ferris Bueller's Day Off*

Trouble is the common denominator of living. It is the great equalizer.
> Ann Landers

Life is a series of crises separated by brief periods of self-delusion.
> Mikey Slavin
> in Richard Rosen's *Fadeaway*, 1986

Life is barren enough; surely with all her trappings, let us, therefore, be cautious how we strip her.

> DR. SAMUEL JOHNSON

Life is what you do/ while waiting to die. Life is how the time/ goes by.

> SONG LYRIC FROM THE BROADWAY MUSICAL *Zorba*

Life is a language in which certain truths are conveyed to us; if we could learn them in some other way, we should not live.

> ARTHUR SCHOPENHAUER

Life is a struggle, but not a warfare.

> JOHN BURROUGHS
> *The Summit of the Years*, 1913

Life can't be all bad when for a few dollars you can buy all the Beethoven sonatas and listen to them for ten years.

> WILLIAM F. BUCKLEY, JR.

Life is like a box of chocolates. You never know what you're gonna get.

> FORREST GUMP'S MOTHER
> in the 1994 motion picture *Forrest Gump*

Life is truly a ride. We're all strapped in and no one can stop it. When the doctor slaps your behind, he's ripping your ticket and away you go. As you make each passage from youth to adulthood to maturity, sometimes you put your arms up and scream, sometimes you just hang on to that bar in front of you. But the ride is the thing. I think the most you can hope for at the end of life is that your hair's messed, you're out of breath, and you didn't throw up.

> JERRY SEINFELD
> *SeinLanguage*, 1993

Life is a sea. We are the ships. Let us go straight to harbor.

> LUCIE CAMPBELL WILLIAMS
> American educator

Life becomes livable only to the extent that death is treated as a friend, never as an enemy.

> MOHANDAS K. GANDHI

The one thing you learn in life is that nobody should win. We just keep playing. One power can rise, the other can fall. There are periods of indolence and apathy. Influences are fluid.

> WILLIAM SAFIRE
> quoted in *Men's Journal*, October 1994

The trick in life is to know what you want after you get it.

> KATHARINE HEPBURN
> in the 1994 motion picture *Love Affair*

Life is like an onion: You peel off layer after layer and then you find there is nothing in it.

> JAMES GIBBONS HUNEKER

That life is meaningless may be a lie, so far as the whole of life is concerned. But it is the truth at any given instant.

> ALDOUS HUXLEY

Life is for each man a solitary cell whose walls are mirrors.

> EUGENE O'NEILL

Just when I found the meaning of life, they changed it.

> GEORGE CARLIN

[Life], in a way, is so banal, that you might as well make a kind of grandeur of it, rather than be nursed to oblivion.

> British artist FRANCIS BACON
> quoted in *The [London] Sunday Times,* 1975

Life resembles a novel more often than novels resemble life.

> GEORGE SAND

Life consists in what a man is thinking of all day.

> RALPH WALDO EMERSON

Life is too short for traffic.

> DANIEL BELLACK

The great secret of life is not to open your letters for a fortnight. At the expiration of that period you will find that nearly all of them have answered themselves.

> ARTHUR BINSTEAD

Life is a crooked labyrinth.

> HENRY KING
> *The Labyrinth*

When people are serving, life is no longer meaningless.
>JOHN GARDNER

Life is a scrambled egg.
>DON MARQUIS

All life is based on decisions. Decide now on what you would like to become and what you would like to do. The two are not necessarily the same, although sometimes they can be.
>LOUIS L'ARMOUR
>*The Lonesome Gods*

Life is pharmaceutical from head to cuticle.
>DAVID McCORD
>*Perambulator Poems*, No. xiv, 1941

Life is a journey, not a destination.
>VARIOUSLY ATTRIBUTED

Life is not a series of gig lamps symmetrically arranged; life is a luminous halo, a semi-transparent envelope surrounding us from the beginning of consciousness to the end.

> Virginia Woolf
> *A Common Reader,* 1925

Life has many disasters and reversals, but only one true tragedy: to pass from infancy to senility without ever reaching maturity.

> Sydney Harris
> in *Presbyterian Journal,* Aug. 15, 1979

I believe we have two lives. The life we learn with, and the life we live after that.

> Glenn Close to Robert Redford
> in the 1984 motion picture *The Natural*

Life is a 440 horsepower in a 2-cylinder engine.

> Henry Miller
> recalled on his death day,
> June 7, 1988

Who can decide offhand which is absolutely better, to live or to understand life? We must do both alternately, and a man can no more limit himself to either than a pair of scissors can cut with a single one of its blades.

> William James

About the Author

Ronald B. Shwartz is a lawyer engaged in the practice of civil litigation. Since 1980 he has been associated with the Boston law firm of Goulston & Storrs, of which he is a Director and Vice President. He is a member of the Massachusetts Academy of Trial Attorneys and other professional organizations, and his practice has been most recently recognized in *Who's Who in American Law* (1993–94). He is a graduate of The University of Chicago Law School, where he served as Articles Editor of *The University of Chicago Law Review*. Mr. Shwartz is also a former freelance writer whose essays and reviews have appeared in *The Wall Street Journal, The Nation, The Los Angeles Times, The American Spectator, The Sewanee Review,* and a wide range of other major periodicals. In 1981 he was admitted to The National Book Critics Circle.